For You

Andreas Seidl

Handover of Power

European Version

Volume 17: Security

Imprint

Bibliographic information of the German National Library: The German National Library lists this publication in the German National Bibliography; detailed bibliographic data are available on the Internet at http://dnb.dnb.de.

© 2022 Dipl. Pol. Theodor Andreas Seidl

Cover: Christiane Ebrecht
Translation: DeepL, Cologne
Production and publishing: BoD – Books on Demand, Norderstedt

ISBN: 978-3-7568-0267-8

Acknowledgements

My thanks go to my family and friends who have made me who I am today. Special thanks to all those who supported me in writing this book. I would like to thank all my classmates, teachers, fellow students, lecturers, demonstrators, activists, colleagues, companies and countries with whom I have had the privilege of sharing the experiences from which all the ideas in this book have emerged. I would like to thank the staff of Books on Demand for their kind helpfulness. I thank the citizens of Seligenstadt for the harmony and solidarity in which I was able to write.

Foreword

This policy concept contains a variety of proposals for possible political reforms. It can be peacefully and democratically adapted to any current political system of any state in the world, but also to political systems in families, clubs, associations or companies. Wherever humans make or submit to rules that manage living together, the following proposals can be helpful. Readers who find the proposals so helpful that they would like to implement them together with like-minded people can contact the author. The contact form on the last page can be used for this purpose.

Faults and defects

I ask for your understanding that this volume was not professionally proofread. I could only afford professional proofreading for the summary. Spelling errors and unfortunate phrasing may therefore occur. As soon as this volume has sold enough to pay for a professional proofreading, it will be done. After that, a new edition will be published.

English version

Please understand that this volume has been translated automatically. I could only afford a professional translation for the summary. Poor wording and spelling errors may therefore occur. In case of doubt, the German version shall prevail. As soon as this volume has sold enough to pay for a professional translation, it will be done. After that, a new edition will be published. It was more important to me that no one in the world should have an information advantage than individual translation errors in the complete work.

References
If something has been quoted directly, it is set in italics. If the headings contain footnotes, the sources for direct and indirect quotations apply in the chapter for which the heading stands. Otherwise, quotations or source references are directly at the word or at the end of the sentence or paragraph. This book contains parts of text based on the Federal Constitution of the Swiss Confederation of 18 April 1999 (as of 12 February 2017), abbreviated to BV[1] and the Constitution of the Canton of Bern of 6 June 1993 (as of 11 March 2015), abbreviated to KV[2] .
If the constitutional paragraph, or individual paragraphs thereof, are based in whole or in part on extracts from the BV or KV, this is indicated in a footnote. The references to the corresponding footnotes for constitutional paragraphs are usually found after the heading of the affected chapter and sometimes in the body of the text. Articles used in the Swiss constitutions are listed in the footnote with a number after the title of the constitutional paragraph. Example: §123 Sample title: BV Art.123, KV Art.123.
All internet sources are fully cited in the footnotes. They were last accessed on 30.09.2021. All literature sources are also listed in full in the footnotes.
All references to tasks undertaken by other ministries and described in more detail there are given in footnotes. Example: Model Ministry - 1.2.3 Model Chapter.
All footnotes are to be viewed in comparison to the respective source, so-called indirect quotations. Direct quotations are set in italics, but hardly ever occur. The source reference is intended to enable further investigation and to take copyright

---

1 This is not an official publication. Only the publication by the Swiss Federal Chancellery is authoritative. https://www.fedlex.admin.ch/eli/cc/1999/404/de On 14.12.2021
2 This is not an official publication. The Bernese Official Collection of Laws is authoritative. https://www.belex.sites.be.ch/frontend/versions/2420?locale=de#ART71 On 16.12.2021

into account.

All keywords used, based on the names of the responsible units, departments and ministries of Germany, are listed at the end of this volume in the chapter on the conversion of ministries.

Table of contents

1 Goals of the Ministry of Security

The fundamental goal of the Ministry of Security is peace. It uses the state's monopoly on the use of force for the benefit of the people and in voting with the people in the most cost-effective way. The use of lethal weapons should be the exception and be replaced by non-lethal weapons as far as possible. If possible, no human should be killed by the security forces. On the other hand, security forces should be able to use minor injuries as a disciplinary measure against verbal or physical attackers. The aim is to generate respect for the monopoly on the use of force, which is basically friendly and helpful. However, anyone who violates the law and defies the legally permissible instructions of the security forces is immediately punished and the handling is characterised by coercive measures permissible under criminal law.

Force is used only as briefly as possible and as violently as necessary. Military deterrence applies only to the protection of external borders. Other states should realise that the military is not designed for the conquest of foreign countries. Peace treaties should thus be easier to achieve. At the same time, the population should be able to defend its democratic freedom of self-determination against occupiers in an emergency.

The short-term goal is the establishment of the European Defence Army. The medium-term goal is the remote control of all weapon systems and an effective defence mechanism against celestial bodies in space. The long-term goal of the Ministry of Security is to abolish border protection, Customs and the military. Only defence systems against celestial bodies are to be maintained. The Ministry of Security supports the discovery and settlement of Earth-like planets with its equipment.

2 Departments

The departments are divided into sub-departments and enumerations are usually considered as their individual units. Many tasks of some departments are completely taken over by other ministries as a service.

2.1 Central Department

Part of the Central Department is the Reception Office with the Courier and Mail Room, which directs all concerns, broadcasts and visitors to the appropriate place in the ministry.

2.1.1 Staff

The Human Resources Department is responsible for staff development and planning. For this purpose, it takes care of the recruitment of junior staff, intern and trainee programmes as well as the selection procedures for employees and special selection procedures for applicants with disabilities. For politicians and employees, the department prepares a job plan. In all its tasks, it works in voting with the personnel board.[1]

All other personnel matters are transferred to the relevant ministries. The Ministry of Education is responsible for the training and further education of employees for the state service.[2] The Ministry of Labour takes over the service law.[3] This includes labour and collective bargaining law for employees in the state service, remuneration, personnel administration of all careers and employees, flexitime, holiday and sick leave, working time with or without flexitime in part-time or full-time at the place of work or in home work. The Ministry of Infrastructure provides housing assistance for all state employees.[4] The Ministry of Finance's Pay Office takes care of employees' salary, expenses, travel and relocation costs.[5] The Ministry of Education provides childcare for all employees in the state service.[6]

The Ministry of Health is responsible for the occupational health service.[7] It ensures occupational health management, deals with the treatment, education and prevention of

---

1 Ministry of State Organisation - 2.1.1.1 Personnel board
2 Ministry of Education - 2.1.1.1 Education and training for the state service
3 Ministry of Labour - 4 State enterprises, 13 Labour Directory
4 Ministry of Infrastructure - 2.1.1.1 Housing assistance for state service employees
5 Ministry of Finance - 2.1.1.1 Staff remuneration
6 Ministry of Education - 2.1.1.2 Childcare for state service employees
7 Ministry of Health - 2.1.1.1 Occupational Health Service

occupational accidents, controls and provides occupational health and safety through the health auditors[8] of the Company Auditing Agency[9] .

2.1.2 Organisation

The ministries of media, justice, finance, labour, state organisation provide audit services for quality management in the ministry, evaluation of work performance, revenues and expenditures, as well as prevention of corruption, protection against sabotage and, if necessary, disciplinary matters.[10]
The Ministry of Labour regulates procurement law and ensures corruption-free state orders and procurement.[11] The Ministry of Finance organises the annual budget vote and ensures proper accounting in each ministry.[12] It regulates budget procedures, budget law, staff budgets, departmental budgets, costs and cash management, and assists ministries in budget planning for the budget vote. The language service for translating talks or texts is provided by the Ministry of Education.[13]
The Ministry of Digital Affairs supports the supply of Information Technology.[14] In voting with the Procurement Office of the Ministry of Labour, it takes care of the procurement, provision, maintenance and service of technical devices and software. Much of this is produced in-house to ensure data protection in information and communication technology. Information technology and digitalisation officers audit and advise the ministries. Digital appointment calendar and documentation services are provided as well as a digital policy archive including a library.

---

8 Ministry of Labour - 20.7.2 Health auditor
9 Ministry of Labor - 20 Company Auditing Agency
10 Ministries of Media, Security, Justice, Finance, State Organisation - 2.1.2.1 Audit services
11 Ministry of Labour - 6 Procurement Office
12 Ministry of Finance - 8 state revenues, 9 state expenditure
13 Ministry of Education - 2.1.3 Language Service
14 Ministry of Digital Affairs - 2.1.2.1.1 Supply of Information Technology

2.1.2.1 Audit services[15]

The Office for the Protection of the Constitution is the audit services of the Ministry of Security, which checks the work of the ministries for their compliance with the Constitution. The police audits the constitutional compliance of citizens, in particular compliance with fundamental rights. Both audit services of the Ministry of Security work with the prosecution offices of the Ministry of Justice to have violations judicially reviewed.

2.2 Management Department

The Management Department is the minister's department. With his office team, he provides policy planning and analysis for his ministry and coordinates the relationship between the nation and the municipality through exchanges with his deputies in the municipalities. He initiates cooperation with other ministries or citizens in committees and is supported by the Ministry of State Organisation.

The Ministry of Media Affairs, through its media service, provides press and public relations for the ministry, moderates civil dialogue, trains or provides a spokesperson for the minister, writes speeches and texts on request, and ensures the implementation of conferences and events.[16]

The Ministry of Digital Affairs is responsible for digital management and thus provides departmental management. It automatically produces business statistics, staff surveys and the current state of research through statistics. It automatically forwards proposals to the affected or empowered state employees. In document management, it ensures digitalisation and that ministries share forms with each other.[17]

---

15 §70.2 Supervision: BV Art.169, §71.4 Review of effectiveness
16 Ministry of Media Affairs - 2.2.1.1 Media Service
17 Ministry of Digital Affairs - 2.1.2.1 Digital Service

2.3 European Department

The Ministry of Foreign Affairs ensures the constant transmission of the latest information on current European policy affecting the ministry concerned, applicable European Union law and all European Union funding programmes starting or in progress.[18]

The European Department is responsible for clarifying policy issues and coordinating the Common Foreign and Security Policy (CFSP) and the Common Security and Defence Policy (CSDP).[19] This includes cross-border law enforcement and prevention of danger by all security forces, joint protection of the European Union's external borders and the European Defence Army. The European Department organises security policy relations with European Union member states in voting with the Security Minister.

The European Department decides for the areas of CSDP[20] , humanitarian aid and disaster management[21] , police and customs cooperation[22] , combating terrorism[23] , combating organised crime[24] , customs cooperation[25] , customs - general rules[26] , customs-specific rules and regulations[27] , tariffs, controls and exemptions[28] , whether to adopt, adapt or reject existing European Union law.[29]

---

18 Ministry of Foreign Affairs - 2.4 European Department

19 https://eur-lex.europa.eu/summary/chapter/25.html?expand=2504#arrow_2504

20 https://eur-lex.europa.eu/summary/chapter/2505.html

21 https://eur-lex.europa.eu/summary/chapter/humanitarian_aid.html?root_default=SUM_1_CODED=04

22 https://eur-lex.europa.eu/summary/chapter/2304.html

23 https://eur-lex.europa.eu/summary/chapter/2307.html

24 https://eur-lex.europa.eu/summary/chapter/2308.html

25 https://eur-lex.europa.eu/summary/chapter/1201.html

26 https://eur-lex.europa.eu/summary/chapter/1206.html

27 https://eur-lex.europa.eu/summary/chapter/1209.html

28 https://eur-lex.europa.eu/summary/chapter/1208.html

29 Ministry of Foreign Affairs - 6.4 Conversion of political contents to the policy of dynamic media democracy

2.4 Security Policy Department

The Security Policy Department is responsible for coordinating all measures affecting all security agencies or organised in cooperation with other ministries. It operates the Security Directory[30] and the Investigation Directory. In the event of an emergency or disaster, it shares selected data from the Security Directory with other affected states in order to coordinate operations. For criminal cases, offences and the control of persons and goods entering and departing the country, it shares the data from the Investigation Directory with states that also share their investigation data to the same extent.

It is responsible for formulating security policy bills. If the rules are to be standardised across Europe or worldwide, it works together with the Ministry of Foreign Affairs.

The Security Policy Department is responsible for organising international cooperation between the security agencies of the involved states, which provide administrative and legal assistance to each other. To this end, it works in voting with the ministers for security and foreign affairs.

2.5 Department for Internal and External Security

The Department for Internal and External Security operates the security agencies, namely the civil defence, rescue service, fire brigade, Technical Relief Agency, People's Protection Service, police and military.

The department takes care of the cooperation and networking of the individual security agencies and the balanced deployment of personnel of all available security forces between all security agencies. It coordinates the security forces of the municipalities for national and international operations.

In the event of a disaster or state of emergency, the Department for Internal and External Security coordinates the division of tasks with all necessary ministries. For this purpose, it can give them instructions necessary to deal with the disaster or state of emergency in voting with the Minister of Security. It conducts regular committees and voting with the population during a

---

30 Ministry of Digital - 12 Directories

disaster or state of emergency to ensure democratic control.

3 Tasks of the Ministry of Security[31]

The Ministry of Security's task is to protect the country's inhabitants and guard the democratic state in which they live. The Ministry of Security is the only ministry, apart from the Ministry of Justice in the penal system, that is allowed to use force. The Minister of Security and his deputies are subject to democratic control.

The security forces have the task of enforcing the law of public safety and order, which is set by the people. The task of the Minister of Security is to maintain internal and external security. To maintain internal security, he is assisted by his deputies in the municipalities. The security forces are staffed and technically equipped in such a way that they are able to ward off dangers and protect the people from attacks, disasters, emergencies and crime independently of other states. The unarmed security forces of the fire brigade, the rescue service and the Technical Relief Agency ward off the dangers of emergencies and disasters. The armed security forces of the Army, Customs, Police and People's Protection Service protect the citizens from crime and attacks from within and outside the country.

The People's Protection Service serves as a domestic security service to protect citizens and companies that feel threatened. The police serve to record and investigate criminal offences and misdemeanours inland and to report them to the Ministry of Justice. The People's Protection Service is subordinate to the police and is subject to police law. Customs controls the movement of persons and goods between inland and foreign countries and collects tariffs. The military is used to ward off dangers from abroad and to support the domestic security forces in peacetime. Wars of aggression are prohibited. Operations inland are only permitted under the authority of the police.

Firstly, military neutrality is guaranteed by not executing wars of aggression and other military foreign missions, but by concluding peace treaties. Secondly, the European Defence

31 §169,1,2,5 Security: BV Art. 173, §173,3 Army

Army serves only to defend the existing external borders of the European Union. Should the case of defence arise, the Security Minister has the task of using violent measures to defend the borders. Should the laws in force not be sufficient to effectively combat danger, attacks or crime, the Security Minister has the task of enforcing urgent projects by means of regulations and decisions for a short period of time until the corresponding legislative process has been completed.

4 Security policy

Security policy regulates all areas in which several security agencies work together. The Minister of Security and his deputies in the municipalities are responsible for security policy and the individual security agencies, such as the police, People's Protection Service, Customs, prevention of danger and the military. The security minister is responsible for security agencies that are only deployed nationally or internationally. The people can decide how they are to be deployed. For security agencies that also or exclusively operate on a municipal level, the deputy minister of security in the respective municipality is responsible. The affected citizens can demand municipal different hardship or leniency, according to their security needs. If other laws apply in a municipality, for example in cultural protection areas, the security agencies enforce these municipal laws.

4.1 Security forces[32]

Security forces are all Ministry of Security workers who work in security agencies such as the Police, People's Protection Service, Customs, Military, Fire Service, Rescue Service and Technical Relief Agency. In order to use security forces personnel as efficiently as possible, security forces are deployed in several different security agencies, depending on their staffing level and qualifications.
These security forces are entitled to restrict fundamental

32§38 Restrictions on fundamental rights: BV Art.36, KV Art.28, §170.1 Civil Courage rights if the law so provides. The laws must clearly define the content, purpose and scope of the restrictive measures. The fundamental right to freedom is usually affected when accident sites or crime scenes are cordoned off, expulsions and house bans are issued, or arrests and detentions take place. The exercise of democratic rights is a fundamental right that can rarely be restricted. It can only be partially restricted in acute emergencies, such as a state of emergency or state of exception[33] for a limited period of time, or in detention[34] . The core content of fundamental rights[35] may not be restricted under any circumstances.

Moral courage is a right that entitles persons to temporarily arrest other persons if they are caught in the act of committing a criminal offence and there is imminent danger due to flight or obscuration. Moral courage is a duty when it comes to providing first aid to humans in distress. Moral courage is subject to the proviso that helpers do not put themselves in danger.

Every measure must be appropriate to the circumstances that trigger it and must be fundamentally designed to protect the lives and health of humans. Restrictions on the fundamental rights of individuals or groups of citizens must be in the interest of the majority of citizens or justified by the protection of the fundamental rights of third parties or by environmental damage that cannot be repaired in a generation.

There must be no private security services because the monopoly on the use of force must lie with the democratically controlled state. Companies or persons who want additional protection buy this service from the People's Protection Service. If 60% of the citizens feel unsafe in an area of 1km radius, they can request a free People's Protection Service patrol from the town hall.

33Ministry of State Organisation - 12.6 State of exception, 12.7 State of emergency
34Ministry of Justice - 7.5.1 Restriction of rights
35§1 Human dignity: BV Art.7, §2 Equality of rights: BV Art.8, §3 Protection against arbitrary state action: BV Art.9, §6 Moral obligations, §7 Personal rights: KV Art.8, §29 General procedural guarantees: BV Art.29, §30 Judicial proceedings: BV Art.30, KV Art.26, §31 Legal protection: KV Art.26, §32 Deprivation of liberty: BV Art.31, KV Art.25, §33 Criminal proceedings: BV Art.32

Only domestic nationals are allowed to work in the police, People's Protection Service, Customs and the military, because it is a sovereign task to hold the monopoly on the use of force, which may only come from the people and may only be controlled by them. In the case of the security forces, the principle applies that anyone who uses force will be subject to the monopoly on the use of force. Anyone who is insolent or violent towards the security forces is immediately punished with a violent response from the security forces. Verbal violence, such as swearing or being cheeky, will be warned the first time it occurs and punished the second time, for example, with pepper spray. Physical violence is punished immediately with arrest. The use of all non-lethal weapons is permitted for arrest if the arrest is resisted and the police file a complaint for violence against security forces[36] . Arrested persons must be handed over to the police immediately if the police has not arrested them themselves.

4.2 Radio communication

All security agencies are equipped with People's Innovation Company Walkie-talkies[37] for the intranet[38] . This device is from the pocket People's Computer series. A special operating system encrypts radio traffic over the intranet.
All emergency services receive the operational information via this connection. The responsible authorities receive satellite images, coordinates, affected persons and locations on their Walkie-talkie.

4.3 Alarm signals

The security forces' vehicles and aircraft are equipped with blue or green circulating light signals during an alert operation. During law enforcement, prevention of danger and emergency medical care operations, blue circulating light signals and a siren consisting of two different horn signals are

36 Ministry of Justice - 8.13.6 Violence against security forces
37 Ministry of Innovation - 10 People's Innovation Company
38 Ministry of Digital Affairs - 13.6.9 Extensions

used to draw attention to the emergency vehicles. During operations for social welfare and disaster management, green circulating light signals and loud music are used. In addition, announcements may be made through the loudspeakers to inform the surrounding population. Alarm sirens on the roof of the town hall are used to announce disaster alerts. By the nature of the signals, the population will know what rehearsed behaviour to adopt.

4.4 Charges against security agencies

Charges against security agencies must be filed with the competent public prosecutor's office, for which the Ministry of Justice is responsible.[39] The accessibility via telephone, address and intranet address must be displayed in every police station for citizens to see.

4.5 Duty of the security agencies to provide information

Security agencies are required, unless they are undercover, to wear their badge number or name visibly on their uniform and to state their legal basis for action when asked by a citizen affected by their action. In the case of coercive measures, the legal basis and the rights for the victims of the coercive measure must be announced.[40]

4.6 Security Directory[41]

The Security Directory consists of profiles of security agencies, groups for individual services and subgroups for individual intervention teams. It is used on the one hand to organise the security forces and on the other hand for supervision by the citizens. Security forces are assigned to the security agencies for which they are deployed through their profiles from the Labour Directory. They organise themselves into groups

39 Ministry of Justice - 5.6.3.1 Charges against security agencies
40 Ministry of Justice - 8.13.3 Duty of security agencies to provide information
41 §169.3 Security: BV Art. 57

corresponding to their colleagues. Further sub-groups are formed for individual cases and assignments. When the case is finished, the subgroup is closed, but the contents are saved and archived.

The sub-groups are closed groups where work reports are filed and duty rosters are filled in and voted on. Citizens do not have access to these contents, but security forces do, provided they are members of the group. Who is to become a member of which group is decided by the central duty roster, but the security forces have a say in this. The Planned Economy duty roster procedure is used for this purpose.[42] The municipalities can request or release security forces through the national alliance.

In order for citizens to be able to exercise their supervision over state organs, the Security Directory shows where which security agencies have offices and what work these offices do. Investigative and personal data are anonymised. If there is a suspicion of violations of the law, a report can be made and anonymity can be revoked in court proceedings. Citizens can easily call on the help of all security agencies via the Security Directory and become volunteers themselves. Especially in the event of a disaster and during disaster management exercises, all citizens receive an overview of which services they are assigned to in which disaster. They can occupy these services according to the roster procedure of the Planned Economy or exchange them with other citizens.

4.7 Weapons law[43]

All lethal weapons and explosives located inland must be entered in the national weapons register. The entry contains the identification number of the weapon, a picture and the contact details of the owner and user. Explosives may be used commercially or for private celebrations, such as New Year's Eve, with the permission of the responsible deputy minister of security. The commercial and private use of explosives is

---

42 Ministry of Planned Economy - 7.6.4 Labour Choice / Labour Demand
43 §223 Weapons and war material: BV Art. 107

monitored by Company Auditing Agency technical auditors so that explosives can cause as little damage as possible, but only serve peaceful purposes.

Lethal weapons and military explosives are only used in hostage situations and by special task forces inland, otherwise only for national defence in case of attack. In general, all lethal weapons are considered weapons of war and are to be used only against foreign countries, if possible, and not against nationals. Exceptions are hostage-taking and when the enemy uses a lethal weapon.

Weapons of war should only serve to defend the external border, i.e. only reach up to 100km into the neighbouring country. If the attacks reach further, persist and a state of siege threatens, superweapons will be used. The superweapons are remote-controlled aerial explosive devices with lasers that destroy all military institutions that continue to attack the external border.

Non-lethal weapons are used by the police and the People's Protection Service inland. These weapons are to be allowed to be used in cases of insult and slight bodily harm and are thus to be used more quickly. There are close combat weapons, such as baton or pepper spray, and long range weapons, such as stun guns, rubber bullets, poison dart launchers, net launchers or drones with non-lethal close & long range weapons.

The production of lethal weapons and weapons of war is manufactured exclusively in specially secured Planned Enterprises of Planned Economy. Other private or corporate production of lethal weapons and ammunition is prohibited. Domestic companies that are able to convert their civilian production to the production of weapons only produce weapons on orders from the Ministry of Security. The necessary weapons production equipment must be stored in secure buildings in barracks. Joint-stock companies are prohibited from producing weapons so that war and hatred do not increase dividends, the value of the company or other finance economy incentives to spread violence and murder.

4.7.1 Sale and possession

Lethal firearms may only be owned and used by the military, police, hunters and members of shooting clubs. Hunters and members of shooting clubs store their weapons at the local police station. The sale of weapons of all kinds and ammunition to holders of a firearms licence also takes place there. Other sale or distribution of firearms is prohibited. Only local police stations serve as storage facilities and shops for weapons and ammunition. The nearest local police stations must be used for purchase and storage so that police officers know the persons in possession of weapons. In the case of previous convictions for violent offences, possession of weapons is prohibited and weapons are refused to be handed over. In the event of a state of emergency where armed force is used, the population will be armed by the police or, if necessary, by the mayor.[44]

4.7.2 Firearms licence

Hunters and members of a shooting club must obtain a firearms licence before owning a firearm. To do so, they must pass an examination in which their knowledge of safety regulations is tested. Holders of a firearms licence must be exempt from punishment prior to their acquisition and during their possession. The motions for and issuance of a firearms licence take place at the local police station in the applicant's place of residence. The firearms licence must be presented by the holder whenever a firearm is lent out or purchased and must be checked by the issuing police officer.

4.8 Large events[45]

Organisers of large events, such as football matches, must order security personnel for the event period for events with a number of 500 persons or more. The number of security forces must be 1% of the number of visitors. The security forces for 500 persons are 5 each from the fire brigade, the emergency

---

44 Ministry of State Organisation - 12.7.7.2.3 Arming the population
45 §20,2,4 Freedom of assembly: BV Art.22

medical services and the People's Protection Service.

Large events are not protected by the police. If the organisers can suspect criminal offences by their visitors, they have to buy the necessary security personnel from the People's Protection Service. If the visitors commit crimes outside the venue, it is considered rioting. On the first incident, the organiser will be warned and given all personal data to permanently exclude the rioters from his events. In the case of the second incident, the organiser must pay for the deployment of all security forces that are alerted in the event of rioting. In the case of the third incident, the organiser loses his permit and has to stop operations. Rioters who riot again after their imprisonment will receive twice as much imprisonment. For visitors who are prepared to use violence, the organiser can provide the space and time for a brawl or the destruction of prepared objects, or visitors can bring things they want to break together. The organiser provides health care for the injured and the immediate removal of rubbish and damage through entrance fees or deposits.

4.9 Demonstrations[46]

If possible, demonstrations should be registered by at least one organiser 3 days before the event at the local police station. Registration is obligatory if the number of participants is expected to exceed 500 persons already 4 days before the demonstration. Persons may assemble in public places for demonstrations at any time, provided that this does not disturb the night peace of residents. If the number of persons involved exceeds 100, at least one of the participants must inform the police so that demonstrators or bystanders can be protected.

Demonstrations are accompanied by a People's Protection Service protection squad in the demonstration procession and escorted by two police vehicles in front and behind the demonstration procession. Additional security forces are only called in if criminal offences are observed. As soon as rioting

---

46§20,1,3 Freedom of assembly: BV Art.22, KV Art.19, §170,1 Civil courage

takes place, the police react accordingly. Demonstrations are primarily protected by the demonstrators. If necessary, organisers assign stewards to secure the demonstration procession. Offenders should immediately be temporarily arrested by other demonstrators. If this is not possible, the police must be informed immediately.

In the case of counter-demonstrations, violent demonstrators are allowed to report to the police, who then cordon off an area where volunteers are allowed to participate in a brawl and pay a participation fee equal to the health costs caused. If counter-demonstrations are registered or observed by security forces, the Ministry of Media Affairs is immediately alerted to take a mediating role.[47]

4.9.1 Violent demonstrations

Peaceful demonstrators are obliged to report offences in a demonstration as soon as possible and, together with other peaceful demonstrators, to temporarily arrest the offender(s) and hand them over to the police. Demonstrators who violate this and do not obey police announcements automatically make themselves accomplices.

In the case of rioting that occurs out of a peaceful demonstration, the demonstration is stopped. Rioters are taken into custody by the police and brought before a magistrate. To prevent rioters from immediately breaking up every demonstration, a demo TV show is held at a time determined by the police on the same day after the final rally, which also includes a solution finder show revolving around the question: How could we have prevented this today? During this show, the arrested people will be connected via video and will be able to express their motives.

---

[47] Ministry of Media Affairs - 7.2.1.2 Demo TV

4.10 State of emergency[48]

A state of emergency is declared in the event of an event organised by humans for the purpose of endangering the state or seizing power. The Ministry of State Organisation regulates in the law how power can nevertheless remain with the people.[49] The state of emergency can be declared by any minister who first learns of it. All ministers then immediately meet in real or digital form as a cabinet to confirm the state of emergency and newly declare it together. Ministers involved in endangering the state or seizing power are expelled and put on the wanted list. In the case of war or a coup, the military is responsible; in the case of civil war and revolts, it is the police. In the event of a coup d'état, all security forces, including arms, are called to join the vigilantes. During a state of emergency, the responsible security agencies and, if necessary, the people, carry out the appropriate measures that have been rehearsed.

4.11 Terrorism

As soon as there is domestic terrorism, the state has done something wrong. Terrorism always occurs when there are humans who are against a current policy that affects them. These humans always initially try to raise their concerns with the politicians who are responsible, through words and deeds. But if the governments refuse to change anything in their policies and never respond to this opposition, however small it may be, terrorism can arise. There are always those in opposition who give up, despair, are broken and resign. But there are also other oppositionists who do not want to give up, but leave the democratic and diplomatic level unsuccessfully and resort to the means that humans used in crises before politics, namely war. But since oppositionists do not have the money for a large army with state-of-the-art weapons, they use guerrilla tactics and carry out attacks that are as unpredictable as possible and cause as much damage as possible. This is then terror for the entire population.

48§172.1 Internal and external security in a state of emergency: KV Art. 91

49Ministry of State Organisation - 12.7 State of emergency

To avoid this, no weapons may be exported from the domestic country and the military may only use its armed force in cases of defence. Any participation in other international military operations is prohibited. Trade policy works with tariffs and import or export restrictions to avoid distress in other countries. This prevents international terror at home.

National terror is avoided by ensuring that all residents of the country enjoy public freedom of speech and that nationals have co-determination rights. Public freedom of speech also means being able to express one's opinion on the street and in the digital space, to hear and discuss approval or disapproval. As soon as a minority of affected citizens has been found, they can trigger an initiative quorum, or move together and form a municipality from 5000 persons. Once a minority of 10% of the nationals have been found, a People's Committee can be applied for at the Ministry of State Organisation. The People's Committees must be held within 6 months of the application and broadcast on Government Television[50] . The People's Committees are attended by the responsible parties with representatives of their wings. All wings seek similarities with the opposition members or offer to open a new wing in their party. National terror is stopped if the potential terrorists can bring their opinion and commitment to a party, cultural protection area or law.

4.12 Social hotspots

The Ministry of Security records places where there is an increase in criminals or where crimes are committed. These places are reported to the town hall. In cooperation with the Ministries of Integration, Infrastructure, Planned Economy and Justice, expulsions are issued and enforced by the police. The People's Protection Service is responsible for resettlements. Criminal or unemployed foreigners are immediately deported or placed in deportation detention if they cannot pay the costs of deportation.[51] Unemployed people are resettled in Social Villages. Humans who work or receive a pension but

50 Ministry of Media - 7 Government Television
51 Ministry of Justice - 8.10.4 Deportations

cannot afford another flat participate in the housebuilding programme[52] and are immediately given the next available flat in the area of their election on a hire-purchase basis. If they cannot move immediately, they live in the Social Village until their new home is ready.

4.13 Memorials

Memorials are established at places where serious crimes were committed that affected the entire people. At memorials, which are left in their original state as far as possible, the crime is described and how much humans suffered as a result. Memorials describe the suffering of the victims of the crime, the motives and suffering of the offenders during their punishment.

Memorials that are not at the place of the events and are to be removed. Inherited guilt is ruled out because it leads to a depressed, despondent and immature population, which would damage democracy in the country.

Memorials are meant to avoid faults that have led to an unsafe situation for the population. Education about motives and methods should be warnings so that the people can free themselves from the guilt of the offenders. This distance is necessary in order not to become an offender oneself, but to exclude similar actions for one's own being, even if one is in the succession of the offenders.

5 Prevention of danger[53]

The prevention of danger consists of the state hospitals, university hospitals, the rescue services, the fire brigade, the Technical Relief Agency[54] and the alliance for disaster management, which coordinates all services for the prevention of danger in various disaster situations.

All security forces of the prevention of danger serve civil defence. They help humans in distress, remove them from

---

52 Ministry of Infrastructure - 5.13 Housebuilding programme
53 §9,1 Right to assistance in emergency situations: BV Art.12, §169,3,5
Security: BV Art. 57, §171,1,3,4 Civil defence: BV Art. 61
54 https://www.thw.de/EN/Homepage/homepage_node.html

danger and care for them until they are physically and mentally able to cope without outside help. They also protect property from destruction and help with reconstruction. Anyone who deliberately puts themselves or others in distress in order to obtain benefits is liable to prosecution.

Civil defence is provided by the municipalities and organised by all deputy security ministers. The aim of the organisation is to distribute the equipment among the municipalities and, if necessary, to be able to pull them together into associations and special forces of different sizes. The state civil defence is operated with permanently employed personnel who have completed the relevant training on the job. It is used wherever voluntary or commercial civil defence is not sufficient to protect the population. Voluntary and commercial civil defence must meet the same minimum requirements as state civil defence. A mixed form of voluntary and state civil defence is possible. The greater the frequency of operations, the more permanent staff are employed. In the social market economy, Non-profit agencies can additionally operate commercial civil defence. All civil protection bodies are obliged to provide service in disaster situations and are coordinated by the Ministry of Security.

5.1 Voluntary civil defence

The security forces in the voluntary civil defence are organised according to the militia principle. Volunteers take on a task in civil defence, continuously train and educate each other, organise examinations and exercises. The equipment is provided by the Ministry of Security. If security forces in civil defence suffer damage or lose their lives, they or their relatives receive the necessary support. Compensation of the same amount is paid for each deployment that represents a loss of earnings for the volunteers. If there are not enough volunteers, nationals who are between the age of majority and retirement age will be required to serve for a period of 3 years. The number of years can be adjusted according to need. In order to distribute the services equitably, the procedure from the Planned Economy is adopted for assigning them to a duty roster.[55]

5.2 Rescue service[56]

All persons are obliged to give first aid to a person in distress. If they do not know how to do this or if they would put themselves in danger, they must immediately make an emergency call. Those who provide first aid can oblige other persons in the vicinity to perform the service. The aim is to assist those in need until the rescue service arrives. Anything else is considered failure to render assistance and is punishable by law.

The emergency call centre forwards the call to the rescue service closest to the scene of the accident. After admitting the patient, rescue services visit the hospitals closest to the scene of the accident. If there is enough time, hospitals that specialise in the illness or injury are visited. Hospitals are operated or supervised by the Ministry of Health. Rescue services are operated or supervised by the Ministry of Security. They are supervised by the relevant auditors of the Company Auditing Agency.[57] The Ministry of Security itself maintains the rescue services of the state hospitals and university hospitals. They consist of ambulances and emergency ambulances. Ambulances are mobile intensive care operating theatres in a vehicle or aircraft. Emergency ambulances are a fleet of a fast vehicle or aircraft with which the emergency doctor moves to the operation site as quickly as possible. The escort vehicle is an ambulance. Voluntary and commercial rescue services also have ambulances equipped for emergency medicine. The emergency call centre orders ambulances or rescue vehicles depending on the injury or illness.

---

55 Ministry of Planned Economy - 7.6 Duty roster
56 §170,2 Civil courage, §171,2 Civil defence: BV Art. 61
57 Ministry of Labour - 20.7.2 health auditor, 20.7.4 technical auditor, 20.7.3 economic auditor

5.3 Fire brigade[58]

There are state fire brigades and voluntary fire brigades, but these are also state-funded. Fire brigades are responsible for fighting accidents involving fire, earth, water and air. Their equipment and vehicles are equipped for these types of accidents. The fire brigades are equipped with extinguishing agent cannons that are supported by a compressed air line and an extinguishing agent line. Depending on the type of extinguishing, an additive of extinguishing agent is mixed with the water in the emergency vehicle, which is carried in separate tanks. Via the compressed air lines, either ambient air or certain fire-retardant gases are sent to the cannon by a compressor. The cannon can be switched between single shots and continuous fire, which tends to spray a jet with little atomisation or shoot a cloud of finely atomised droplets.

In the case of state fire brigades, the entire staff consists of employees of the Ministry of Security who are always on standby. These firefighters are also responsible for ensuring adequate preventive fire protection at buildings and events. In voting with the Minister of Safety, they formulate the rules for preventive fire protection and chimney sweeping, which they are also responsible for controlling. The controls consist of requirements that Company Auditing Agency technical auditors apply and controls that builders must order for building plans and event organisers must order for event plans from the fire service. For Barter Economy, Planned Economy and Social Market Economy builders and event organisers, these services are Tax-funded.

The fire brigade is responsible for the operation and utilisation of the services of other civil defence bodies, such as the Water Rescue Service and the Technical Relief Agency, if the emergency requires it.

---

58 §170,2 Civil courage, §171,2 Civil defence: BV Art. 61

5.3.1 Voluntary fire brigade

Volunteer fire brigades consist only to a small extent of employees of the Ministry of Security and to a large extent of voluntary firefighters who are pursuing their profession and are called to a fire brigade station when needed. Employers in the Barter Economy, Planned Economy and Social Market Economy are required to release employees who are in the voluntary fire service from service. Free Market Economy employers may do so voluntarily. Employers will be paid the hourly wage of the absent employee for their time off. That employee's wages should not be reduced as a result of serving on the voluntary fire brigade.

5.3.2 Water rescue

The Wasserwacht protects the population during water sports and the commercial use of water bodies. It specialises in rescuing persons and objects from bodies of water. It leads operations in which humans and things have to be rescued from bodies of water. Its operational vehicles are boats and diving equipment for inland waters and ships and submarines for seas.

6 Technical Relief Agency[59]

The Technical Relief Agency is equipped with various vehicles and machines to provide the infrastructure for operations with many victims or emergency personnel. This includes, for example, pumps, water treatment plants, power generators, lighting systems, excavators, cranes and mobile supply and housing buildings. The Technical Relief Agency mainly uses military equipment for this purpose during peacetime. Expendable devices of the Ministry of Infrastructure can additionally be requested by the Technical Relief Agency for operations. The Technical Relief Agency is either requested by the fire brigade as reinforcement or sent to disaster areas by the Ministry of Security. Most of the Technical Relief Agency's staff are volunteers. Soldiers who are trained to carry

---

59 §170,2 Civil courage, §171,2 Civil defence: BV Art. 61

out equipment in the event of war operate it for the Technical Relief Agency in peacetime.

6.1 People's Work Service

The People's Work Service serves firstly to assign the population in advance to services that must be performed in the event of a disaster. Secondly, the People's Work Service is used to make preparations for natural disasters. People's Work Service takes place within the framework of the People's Service[60] and may also require older citizens to serve for a short period of time for training purposes.

For example, dams, riverbeds, drainage lakes or underground water reservoirs are built against floods. At the same time, these precautions also protect against droughts.

Drainage lakes always have a dam all around and a long shallow sandy beach. In the event of a flood, bathing is prohibited and the entire sandy beach up to the dam is flooded. The water level in the outlet lake is supported by a riverbed that contains several sluices. Each riverbed flows into a natural river. At the mouth is the first sluice. The second sluice is located in front of the outlet lake. As long as there is no high water, the riverbed is dry. During high water, both sluices are opened so that the lake can fill up.

Drainage lakes are built near cities and around large towns through which rivers run. They serve as a free recreational area for residents outside disaster situations of flood or drought.

In densely built-up areas, it will be necessary to build underground water pipes and water storage facilities. These facilities can be used to store drinking water or as underground swimming pools.

---

60 Ministry of Education - 10 People's Service

6.2 Emergency number 110[61]

The Ministry of Security can be reached around the clock, seven days a week on the domestic telephone number 110. Callers can report accidents or crimes here. Every person is obliged to call the emergency number or contact it via the internet or intranet in case of first aid measures or provisional arrest. Every call and call to the website is automatically traced to show the location of the caller. Binding to this is the forwarding to the responsible police station. The police officer handling the call or call has the emergency form on the Ministry of Security's intranet site in front of him. This form also creates a profile for the case in the Security Directory. All the caller's details can be entered here. The telephone call is automatically recorded and saved in the emergency form. All citizens can also fill out this form themselves via their People's Computer in order to call for help inland. On the home page of the Ministry of Security and on the home page of the Security Directory, there is a button that says "Help!". For digital crimes or military attacks, the police offer add-on applications for internet browsers and in the People's Navigator this add-on application is part of the browser by default.

The form is automatically sent to the responsible offices that the police officer selects as responsible on the phone. To the right of the form on the screen, all services of the Ministry of Security are listed. Multiple transmissions to several services are possible.

The police are called in as soon as crimes or accidents on traffic routes are reported. The People's Protection Service is requested as soon as a social emergency call is received and life assistance has to be provided, such as a move to the nearest Social Village. The rescue service is requested as soon as medical assistance is needed. The fire brigade is requested as soon as destruction has to be stopped and removed. Customs is called in as soon as border protection offences are involved. The military is deployed if a military attack is reported. From abroad, nationals can call for help via 0049 110. The embassies and consulates in the caller's respective foreign country will provide fast and unbureaucratic assistance. For

61 §170,1,2 Moral courage

this purpose, the Ministry of Security cooperates with the Ministry of Foreign Affairs. The telephone counselling service is connected to the caller in case of psychological problems. The Ministry of Family Affairs is responsible for the telephone counselling service.[62] The Technical Relief Agency can only be requested by security agencies themselves.

6.2.1 Identity card with emergency function

Every domestic identity card has this emergency function. If you bend a corner and pull it out, a contact is triggered and an emergency call is sent out. Then the identity card expels a radio signal for one minute, which is located by surrounding broadcasters and satellites. An emergency call is automatically sent to the police. This contains the personal data of the identity card holder and the coordinates of the location as well as the direction of movement during the minute the expulsion sends the signal. The emergency function can only be used once. Afterwards, the identity card must be replaced.

6.3 Disaster management[63]

The Minister of Security is responsible for crisis management and civil protection in the event of a disaster. All measures are temporary for the period from the disaster to the initial state. The situation centre is located in the nearest intact town hall for local disasters, in the disaster area for regional disasters and in the capital city of the Ministry of Security for nationwide disasters.
The Minister of Security is responsible for raising the regional and national disaster alert. Deputy security ministers are responsible for sounding the local disaster alarm. After the disaster alarm has been triggered, the measures of the corresponding emergency plans, which have usually been practised with the population, are implemented. Economic freedom may be partially or fully restricted in view of the

---

62Ministry of Family Affairs - 6.2 Cure of souls
63§211 National supply: BV Art. 102

situation. Affected persons are to be supported in such a way that they can shut down their companies without suffering from hunger or homelessness. Loss of rent or income cannot be claimed for this period. All orders can be cancelled free of charge. In voting with the people, compensation payments can be made through tax funds.

The Ministry of Security commissions risk analyses for possible disasters from the responsible institutes of the ministries before the disasters occur. The risk analyses should show approximately how long the disaster will last and when it will cause what damage to which persons and companies. At the beginning of a disaster, the appropriate risk analysis is published and filmed by Government Television. Persons and companies should already know at the beginning of a disaster whether and how they could be affected and for how long. The living situation and gainful employment can then be adjusted accordingly by the citizens. The Ministry of Security uses the risk analyses to develop appropriate emergency plans.

6.3.1 Disaster situations

Disasters can be triggered by nature or humans. Persons and companies that trigger disasters are held accountable.[64] Man-made disasters can be triggered by war, trade restrictions, economic failures, crimes or accidents. Natural disasters are usually floods, inundations, droughts, storms and earthquakes. Accidents caused by persons or companies, which are more common, are fires. World-wide disasters are huge volcanic eruptions, tsunamis, epidemic new diseases, meteorite impacts, solar storms or pole reversals.

6.3.2 Mobilisation

The disaster management receives a damage report of affected persons and buildings from the local rescue forces. It immediately requests all surrounding emergency forces to deploy immediately. The entire civil defence can be

---

64 Ministry of Justice - 8.13.5 Triggering disasters

deployed for disaster management, with the Technical Relief Agency playing the decisive role in setting up the necessary infrastructure. The Ministry of Security is responsible for supporting the affected population with essential goods and services for the duration of the disaster. It is supported by the Ministries of Barter Economy and Planned Economy.[65] The Social Villages provide emergency shelter, food, clothing, building materials, collect donations in kind with the help of the Social Service and provide transport for persons and goods to the disaster areas. The Technical Relief Agency provides sufficient electricity, water and waste disposal. The Barter Economy only comes into play when a disaster has destroyed the power supply and digital devices. Each Barter Economy Zone[66] sends most of its residents into the country as trainers to adapt lifestyles. Families with children under the age of 10 move into the Barter Economy Zone and are trained by the remaining 'indigenous' people to survive without electricity and digitalisation.

Advertisements are placed on state television immediately after the disaster alarm is sounded to encourage citizens to participate in the relief effort. At the same time, a new profile is opened in the Security Directory for this disaster case, with which all damage reports of those affected can be entered and documented on the intranet via People's Computer. Donations of money and goods can be handed in at any town hall. Voluntary labour can be entered in a calendar at the town hall or via the People's Computer. Once enough citizens within a 20km radius have gathered, a bus transfer will be organised from the town hall. Depending on the damage reported by the rescue forces, lists will be handed out to the voluntary helpers as to what tools they could bring with them in order to be able to provide better help on the spot. The moving in of the emergency forces into the disaster area takes place under the sound of loud music. It should be clear to all those affected that the situation is now changing for them. Every 5 minutes the announcement is made: "Reinforcements have arrived!"

---

65 Ministries of Planned Economy and Barter Economy - Disaster management
66 Ministry of Barter Economy - 6 Barter Economy Zone

6.3.3 Emergency plan[67]

Emergency plans are drawn up for all known and multiple possible disasters in which many citizens are affected. Here, those affected are shown all the steps they have to go through and which they can also sue for if necessary. The steps are worked out in detail from noticing the disaster to restoring the initial state. All state and citizen participation in the operation, the organisation by the Ministry of Security and the right to assistance by disaster management in the case of many affected citizens, are included. This elaboration is done in a committee.[68] Affected people from a past disaster are invited to the broadcast as an audience and can participate as spectators. The best solution is sought on how to behave during the disaster and afterwards, what measures are expected from the state and the population. The aim is to develop guidelines for action before disasters occur and to make the effects of disasters as entertaining as possible for all those affected.

Each emergency plan is prepared as a draft by the Ministry of Security in voting with other affected ministries, negotiated in a committee and then regularly rehearsed with the population. At the first rehearsal, all persons can wish which role they would like to have. The computer programme of the Planned Economy's digital duty roster is used for this.[69] There, all persons are linked with their roles and stored in lists. This is followed by another committee, which evaluates the rehearsal, can make changes and have a new rehearsal carried out. In the final dress rehearsal, the emergency plan is rehearsed with all citizens and put to a vote of the people the following week.

The Ministry of Security prepares emergency plans for different scenarios. In these emergency plans, all citizens and companies of the Barter Economy, Planned Economy and Social Market Economy are assigned tasks for different crisis scenarios. The emergency plans are elaborated in committees with the affected citizens. The preparation should not take place in times of crisis and the execution should be practised

---

67 §172.3 Internal and external security in a state of emergency
68 Ministry of Media Affairs - 7.2.3.5 Solution Finder (Legislation Committee)
69 Ministry of Planned Economy - 7.6.1 Digital duty roster

at least once in 10 years. In times of crisis, it is permitted to adapt the emergency plans to the current situation if the situation deviates from the elaborated and tested scenarios. The adjustments make it easier for the population to change what has been rehearsed, rather than having to learn new things in times of crisis without ever having rehearsed them.

6.3.4 Reconstruction

For the deployment of craftspersons, at least one employee is released from service from all construction craft enterprises in Planned Economy and Social Market Economy throughout the country to join the disaster area for a week to help, celebrate and sleep alongside the volunteers. The Ministry of Social Market Economy coordinates the deployment of entire craft companies along with their construction vehicle and tools. Free Market Economy companies can do this voluntarily.

6.3.4.1 Emergency catalogue

An emergency catalogue is provided for all items that are not available as donations in kind. The emergency catalogue includes all the necessary goods to run a household, from building materials and furnishings to clothing and consumer goods, but no food. Each product exists only once and is always similar to the picture and not a specific type. For the products in this emergency catalogue, companies can apply at any time to be contacted in an emergency to negotiate prices. These price negotiations are broadcast in real time on Government Television. The aim is to achieve the lowest possible prices with a high number of buyers and low logistical effort. In addition, companies can achieve a charitable advertising effect here. Regardless of whether buildings are to be built or furnished, the affected citizens buy in bulk and thus achieve lower prices, which the Ministry of Security pays and those affected pay back in instalments. The aim should be to spend donations in kind and otherwise provide replacements as cheaply as possible in order to spare the monetary donations.

6.3.5 Local disasters

When a disaster affects at least 10,000 citizens, a local emergency is declared. The emergency services call on residents and neighbours in the city to help the affected citizens now, together with the emergency services. The town hall of the affected citizens is organising the allocation of cash and in-kind donations. The operation should be completed in one or two days, but after 7 days at the most. In the evening, loud music will be played loudly for one hour from 9pm to 10pm using the loudspeakers on the Ministry of Security's emergency vehicles. Every 20 minutes the announcement is made: "The people say thank you!"

In the event of a local disaster that makes an area uninhabitable for a short time, affected people can be evacuated from the disaster area and distributed to the Social Villages. In the meantime, a mobile Social Village can be built in the disaster area. Once completed, the affected people move in and live there while they do reconstruction work. So in the event of a local disaster, the Social Village comes to the citizens.

6.3.6 Regional disasters

As soon as a disaster affects at least 100,000 citizens, a regional disaster emergency is declared. In the case of a regional disaster that makes a region uninhabitable for a short time, the affected citizens move into the surrounding Social Villages. There, they receive instruction from the craftspersons on what crafts they will do together when they return. Once the disaster area is accessible again, the residents can return to their homes. Housing containers are set up for houses that are no longer habitable. Businesses that are needed in the building trade and forestry operations pack up their tools and move into containers of a mobile Social Village located in the disaster area. The containers only have living quarters and operating rooms for the craftspersons. All containers of the mobile Social Villages are placed in places in the disaster area with inadequate supplies. The craftspersons, together with disaster management, volunteers and those affected, restore the initial situation as quickly as possible.

They are brought to the disaster area by shuttle buses. Buses with volunteers from all over the country set off at fixed times so that they arrive together at the operation site. The buses are loaded with donations in kind and supplies from the volunteers in their cargo compartments. The arrival of the buses resembles a procession and is accompanied by a People's Motor Vehicle[70] who play loud music during the entry, similar to the entry of a People's Committee[71] . The People's Motor Vehicle is set up at suitable places. During the day, it is used as a television studio to report on the disaster and advertise for help. In the evening, it is used as a mobile dance hall. From 8 p.m. to 10 p.m., music is played loudly that can be heard in the crisis area. Every 40 minutes the announcement is made: "The people say thank you!" Loud music sounds from the outside loudspeakers. There are also loudspeakers in the glass container, but they are smaller so that the mobile dance venue cannot disturb the peace. People's Motor Vehicles are set up at large residential collection points for volunteers. The idea is to help during the day, party in the evening and sleep at night. Buses shuttle constantly, bringing new volunteers here and old volunteers home. This shuttle service will only be stopped until the initial factual condition of all those affected has been restored. Persons cannot recover more quickly or rise from the dead, nor can personal belongings be retrieved. Necessary furnishings, on the other hand, can. Donations in kind and money are requested for these items. Monetary donations will be used in the operation for orders from the emergency catalogue and remaining amounts will be distributed to the victims after the operation. The expenses of the Ministry of Security are covered first, and then the remaining amount is paid out to affected people. During the operation, all expenses are handled by the Ministry of Security and financed through

---

70 Ministry of Media - 7.1.1 People's Motor Vehicle
71 Ministry of State Organisation - 9.6.3.4 Moving in

an unlimited emergency loan from the Central Bank.

6.3.7 Continental and global disasters

Disasters that affect the whole country usually also affect the whole continent or the whole world. In such disasters, countries usually act on their own first, because international voting on the course of action takes too long. The Ministry of Security therefore develops scenarios that make the country's action appear non-arbitrary to other countries. This means that cooperation can also take place in times of crisis if the course of action is already agreed upon beforehand. During the usually prolonged catastrophic situation, politicians must praise the population as often as they admonish it. Quick and precise adaptability is to be praised and rewarded by decorations or monuments. Faults in unforeseen situations are to be asked for forgiveness and understanding is to be shown for differently affected sections of the population. It is important to keep the morale of the population upbeat in order to be able to endure the usually protracted consequences of major catastrophes.

6.3.8 Scenarios

The Ministry of Security develops measures for different disaster scenarios and involves the Ministries of Barter Economy and Planned Economy in the planning. The planning results in emergency plans that are voted on with citizens and regularly rehearsed so that citizens know immediately what to do in an emergency.

The Ministry of Security is given admission to stockpiles, capacities and blueprints to determine which items can be damaged or destroyed by water, temperature or radiation and how they are repaired after damage. To do this, the Ministry of Security works with the Company Auditing Agency's auditors for health, technology, innovation and legality. In the Company Auditing Agency's audits, buildings and objects are checked and catalogued for their durability in disaster situations. With this data, the Algoracle[72] can simulate various scenarios.

The country can be hit by various natural disasters. These are natural disasters with local, regional, national or global impact. Local natural disasters are storms, floods, earthquakes, storm surges, landslides, avalanches, volcanic eruptions or tsunamis. National and, due to the interconnected world, usually also global disasters are pandemics, severe volcanic eruptions and meteorite impacts, solar storms and pole reversals.

The end of all scenarios is the same. A weekend-long folk festival is celebrated throughout the country. 12 months after the disaster, a committee is held to discuss what went well, what went badly and what could be improved. The committee also decides on amnesty for detainees who are liable under criminal laws enacted to deal with the disaster.

6.3.8.1 Pandemics

Pandemics are novel pathogens that spread uncontrollably around the world. Handling pandemics is different from handling the other disasters. The Ministry of Health declares the extraordinary situation due to the pandemic.[73] The Ministry of Security works closely with the Ministry of Health and serves as a fulfilment agent with a large contingent of mobile personnel and material.

The emergency plan will be developed jointly between the ministries of health and safety and the people, and updated jointly as necessary during the pandemic.

The Institute for Diseases and Vaccines is responsible for the requirements on appropriate protective measures, equipment, tests, medicines and vaccines, as well as the ongoing measurement and publication of the current incidence of infection.[74]

If the number of infections is high, the Ministry of Security can prescribe the wearing of protective equipment and levy

---

72 Ministry of Digital Affairs - 15.3 Algoracle
73 Ministry of Health - 4.2 Exceptional situation
74 Ministry of Health - 4.5.2.1 Tasks during a pandemic

monetary fines for violations. Depending on the number of infections, stronger or weaker protective measures are taken regionally. If capacities in hospitals reach their limits, hospitals become intensive care units and receive additional containers for health centres and homes of the mobile Social Villages[75] . In cooperation with the Health Agency, the introduction of appropriate protective measures in companies and public places is implemented. Controversial issues regarding protective measures, medicines and vaccinations are clarified in a committee.

6.3.8.1.1 Initial phase

A pandemic is considered to have been reached as soon as 50 persons per 100,000 inhabitants have fallen ill. As soon as chains of infection can no longer be traced and no demonstrably suitable protection and testing options are yet available, all citizens must be placed in domestic quarantine for 4 weeks. All citizens are divided into risk groups according to how likely they are to contract the disease. All citizens who belong to a risk group or are unable to protect themselves adequately will remain in domestic quarantine until infection levels fall below the pandemic mark or appropriate protective equipment is available. Voluntary citizens can report to the Social Service to support citizens in a risk group. They receive special paid leave for this.

6.3.8.1.2 Trace infection chains

Health Agencies handle contact tracing and care for humans in quarantine. In order to track chains of infection, citizens must scan a QR code with their People's Computer if they are there for more than 10 minutes or unprotected with other humans who do not live with them in the household. The QR Code is either placed by organisers at the venue or, if there is no commercial organiser, a QR Code can be generated with a People's Computer, which is then scanned by all other persons

---

75 Ministry of Planned Economy - 19 Mobile Social Villages

in the group. The scanning is done when the group gathers and when they separate. After the pandemic, all this data is deleted. All data may only be used for contact tracing to trace infection chains.

6.3.8.1.3 Conversion of production

During a pandemic, economic freedom is interfered with. While some companies are condemned to stand still, others are forced to convert their production or to market their developments under licence. All suitable companies can be forced by the Ministry of Security to convert their production until the pandemic is over.

The Planned Economy converts its production in the luxury supply work area to the production of missing medical supplies. The Social Service supplies the affected agencies. All companies that are suitable convert their production to the production of tests, medicines, vaccines, protective and disinfection equipment. As soon as the need is met, individual companies take over the production of supplies on a temporary basis, alternating with all other companies, until the pandemic is over.

Developers of tests, medicines or vaccines can be forced to license. This also applies to providers of devices that are necessary to adapt production conditions. The companies that have done the research and development must have their new product produced under licence and can also produce it themselves. The aim is to convert a large part of the pharmaceutical industry available in the country to tests, medicines and vaccines. If distribution difficulties arise, priority is given to the development and production of a vaccine.

All research tasks are adapted to the pandemic at short notice.[76] The companies that are forced to produce something specific for the pandemic are allowed to set a price for it that is 10% above the production costs of the product. If they produce something under licence, 40% of this 10% above the production cost goes to the licensor as a licence fee. Forced

76 Ministry of Innovation - 5.4 State research projects

companies are thus considered to be compensated.

6.3.8.1.4 Test, vaccinate and treat

All stationary and mobile Innovation Labs are converted into test labs and vaccination centres and set up throughout the country by the Social Service. There, the security forces of the prevention of danger, the People's Protection Service and the Social Service test and vaccinate the population nationwide in large car parks.

The family doctors take over the educational talks and the diagnostics for suitability for vaccination. After the interview, they issue a vaccination release for the patient, where they can specify the vaccine, the dose and the dates. The vaccination release with all the data is stored by the GP in the Health Directory on the patient's profile. The vaccination itself can take place at a vaccination centre, doctors' surgeries and hospitals as soon as the vaccination clearance is available. All tests and vaccinations are charged to the Health Card and stored in the Health Directory. Vaccinations must not be compulsory. Unvaccinated persons must not be disadvantaged unless triaging occurs.[77] Refusal to vaccinate despite GP approval for vaccination is considered suicide in demonstrably overcrowded ICUs. The Institute for Diseases and Vaccines makes requirements as to which patients are excluded from treatment and when.[78] Just as crucial as the development of a vaccine is the development of suitable treatment options.

6.3.8.1.5 Research and development

All state medical research institutions, such as institutes, educational institutions and university hospitals, immediately start developing a vaccine, medicine and rapid tests. The majority develop suitable test procedures at the beginning. Once tests are developed, they are manufactured by all suitable companies. Immediately after test development, all

------

77 Ministry of Health - 5.4.4 Triaging
78 Ministry of Health - 4.5.2.1 Tasks in a Pandemic

researchers develop a vaccine or vaccines. Once the first test phase of a vaccine is completed, suitable companies produce it. Immediately after vaccine development, medicines are developed and existing data from hospitals are used. After that, the disease and its long-term course are researched as closely as possible. All hospitals are obliged to report all data via the Health Directory from the beginning of the pandemic. This data is then analysed to research disease progression, late effects and effective treatment methods. Hospitals, physicians and pharmacists have the right to develop their own medicines and treatment methods and to test them on voluntary test patients. They send these studies via the Health Directory to the Institute for Diseases and Vaccines. There, researchers are commissioned to research successful methods, share them with all treating physicians and make large quantities available with the pharmaceutical industry. As soon as a mutation occurs, the tests, medicines and vaccinations are checked for their effectiveness. If they are no longer effective, the measures are repeated to develop tests, medicines or vaccines.

6.3.8.1.6 Final phase

Once all humans in the country have the opportunity to receive a vaccination or acquire protective equipment, the protective measures that restrict personal rights will be lifted. Once the population can be vaccinated or recovered and immune faster than the pathogen mutates, the pathogen can be eradicated. The pandemic is considered to have ended when no more than 50 infected persons per 100,000 inhabitants are recorded in a disease wave and 60 to 80% of the population are immune as a result of vaccination or illness. The extraordinary situation is ended and the state of emergency is lifted.

6.3.8.2 Severe volcanic eruptions and meteorite impacts

In case of severe volcanic eruptions or meteorite impacts, the cities will be converted into Social Villages to support the citizens according to the rules of Planned Economy. The

Social Village centres are placed in the cities by container cross modules[79] . The Ministry of Security confiscates stocks, buildings and blueprints and hands them over to the Ministry of Planned Economy to maintain basic supply. The Planned Economy applies throughout the country in this disaster. Everything that is used to ensure the basic supply of the entire population is administered by the Ministry of Planned Economy and is considered the property of the people. All persons are given a duty roster that assigns them to compulsory work for basic supply. Economic freedom is suspended. All companies convert their production to ensure basic supply. All other companies that cannot contribute to this must close down and release their staff for compulsory work. If there are enough workers and companies for basic supply, other companies can reopen or do not have to close. These companies operate under the conditions of the luxury supply work area in the event of a disaster and are considered Planned Enterprises.

6.3.8.3 Solar storms and pole reversals

During solar storms and pole reversals, the Barter Economy limits the effects of the failure of all electrical devices by means of an electromagnetic shock wave. The Barter Economy lives permanently without electricity and plastic and supports itself with renewable resources. In the event of an emergency, these residents will pass on their knowledge to the rest of the population. From the residents of the Barter Economy, the population learns what to do to survive together on the land without electricity and internet.

The entire country is in Planned Economy and follows the same procedures as severe volcanic eruptions and meteorite impacts. In addition, resettlement is taking place. Families from the cities move to the Barter Economy Zone until the capacity there is exhausted. The original residents of the Barter Economy Zone are resettled in the new Social Villages to set up the electricity-less basic supply together with the Ministries of Security and Planned Economy. A few experienced Barter

79 Ministry of Infrastructure - 5.9 Mobile City

Economy Zone residents remain there and train all the new residents.

6.3.8.4 Uninhabitable Earth Surface

Due to radioactive contamination of humans or air pollution after a severe volcanic eruption or meteorite impact, life on the Earth's surface can be life-threatening for a certain period of time. During this time, disaster management enables the population to survive underground until the earth's surface is habitable again.

6.3.8.4.1 Habitat

There are four tunnel tubes in the tunnel network.[80] One tube is used as a transport tube for goods and persons. In another tube, there are wagons with containers for sleeping, toilet, shower and clothing. In the third tube there are wagons with containers for cooking and eating, washing and logistics, living and playing. In the fourth tube, containers for safety and health as well as education and work alternate. Supply lines for electricity, fluids and data run alongside the four tunnel tubes. These supply lines can be tapped. There are special tools and materials for the installation, which are stored in the storage rooms next to the laundromat.

The ends of the tunnel tubes support the tunnel system with water and electricity. The tunnel tubes end at coasts of seas and lakes at the edge of mountains that are connected to a river. Nuclear power plants are installed at these ends with fuel elements for 200 years, which are only used in emergencies. The tunnel tubes connect the nuclear power plants, lakes and seas. The nuclear power plants are built so that they can be cooled by rivers or the sea. The power plants provide enough electricity to desalinate and purify seawater, treat wastewater and filter air, produce oxygen, generate light, boil steel and manufacture glass. For this case of long-term supply, there are plans where tunnels can be dug to use existing mines for

---

80 Ministry of Infrastructure - 6.2 Underground networks

underground agriculture[81] or to extract mineral resources. Special machinery from mining and tunnelling will be stored for this purpose.

Old mines and bunkers are used for government, heavy industry and underground farming. All these facilities must be connected to the tunnel tube system.

6.3.8.4.2 Life in a container

All tunnels in the country are converted into shelters for the citizens in case of a disaster. To mitigate a disaster that affects the entire country, the tunnel networks[82] will be converted into living space. The trains of the tunnel railway will be equipped with many additional ISO containers. As initial equipment, all mobile Social Villages will be loaded onto the wagons of the tunnel railway and converted accordingly. The following 40-foot or 20-foot containers will be prepared for this purpose.

Sleep
The sleeping containers fit 5 beds in a row and 4 beds on top of each other, so there are 20 beds against each wall, making 40 beds per container and a 50cm wide corridor between the beds. Under each bed is a 10cm high lockable drawer for clothes and personal belongings. Half the number of beds of the total population should be kept in stock at all times. These are all beds that are owned by the state, such as those in Social Villages or hospitals. It is important that these beds are standardised to be stacked on top of each other. In an emergency, all citizens must sleep two to a bed or take turns. Sleeping containers are not walk-through containers. They have doors on both sides, but one side is usually locked and can only be opened in an emergency.

Showers and changing rooms
The open door leads to a small ISO container with lockers,

---

81 Ministry of Labour - 19.8.8 Agriculture away from nature: Indoor agribusiness
82 Ministry of Infrastructure - 8.8.4 Tunnel railway

a changing room and a shower on each side of the wall. The shower cubicle has a mirror, soap dispenser and fold-out washbasin on the wall. There are two concealed power sockets on the ceiling.

Each locker has a bag for dirty laundry. A number is worked into each piece of laundry to identify the owner. The locker is emptied as soon as the bag is full but can still be closed. Full laundry bags are hung to the left of the entrance to this container, and the same bags with the washed laundry hang to the right. The bags also bear the identification number and are washed.

WC

Another small ISO container houses WCs and washbasins with mirrors. There are 2 washbasins next to the entrance door. There are 6 lockable WC cubicles on the right and left wall.

Cooking and eating

A large ISO container is used for storing food, preparing food and drinks, consuming them and cleaning cutlery.

Washing and logistics

A large ISO container is used as a launderette and storage room.

Life and play

Two small ISO containers can be equipped with everything that 80 residents of a container want to spend their free time. For this purpose, there is a catalogue of toys, fitness equipment and entertainment media as well as a uniform annual budget.

Health and safety

Three large ISO containers will each be equipped as a police station with detention cells, a hospital ward with operating theatre and quarantine bed chambers.

Education and work

One large ISO container will be equipped as a seminar room with height-adjustable tables and chairs as well as digital working facilities with admission to the intranet. The other will be equipped with tools and machines from a catalogue by work groups to produce and administer necessary goods in workshops or offices.

6.3.8.4.3 Use of the containers outside the disaster situation

Outside of this disaster, all containers are used for prisons[83] , mobile cities[84] and Social Villages[85] and are only moved into the tunnels in the event of a disaster. The containers for sleeping, showering, changing and WC are used as state hostels in tunnel garages under major cities. All different containers are rented out for events, with staff if desired. All containers are under the responsibility of the Ministries of Infrastructure and Planned Economy outside of disaster situations. The containers are produced in the industrial community Containerbau[86] . For smaller disasters that do not affect the entire population, the containers are moved above ground to disaster areas inland.

6.3.9 International disaster management

The aim of international disaster management is to earn money to keep the material in new and operational condition. The costs are the operation and maintenance costs plus 10% profit. The benefit is adapted to the disaster case and can be granted as a credit.
In order to be able to pump out floods or extinguish forest fires, the industrial community infrastructurators[87] build special devices that are sent into national use as hovercrafts or ocean liners together with heavy-duty zeppelins for water pipes and are lent out internationally for a fee.

---

83 Ministry of Justice - 7.5.5 Prison building
84 Ministry of Infrastructure - 5.9 Mobile City
85 Ministry of Planned Economy - 19 Mobile Social Villages
86 Ministry of Infrastructure - 5.11 Container construction
87 Ministry of Infrastructure - 5.10 Infrastructurators

In order to be able to evacuate refugees, ocean liners are loaded with disaster management containers that are not needed at the moment but must be available in case of emergency. States can decide which services they want to book.

All states that can request and pay for the aid will be granted this aid, unless it is the domestic that needs the aid itself. In the event of a domestic disaster, all refugees must leave the ocean liners and the infrastructure will be reloaded and shipped back inland. If a disaster is suspected, the Ministry of Security can immediately order all aid back inland.

6.3.9.1 Accommodation for the population

The ocean liners are moved to the coast or port closest to the disaster area. There, the necessary infrastructure is unloaded to evacuate the population. The ocean liner will be converted into a floating hotel. A shuttle service will be instituted with vehicles or planes to transport the domestic population to the disaster area. This way, the domestic people can do reconstruction work immediately without having to look for short-term accommodation first. Children will continue to be educated on the ocean liners and those unable to work will be assigned to household chores.

6.3.9.2 Accommodation of the population and reconstruction

The crews of the ocean liners unload all the living containers and build a settlement on the coast. While the refugees move into the living containers and erect more tents under the guidance of rescue workers, the ocean liners leave the operation site again for the home country. Here, infrastructurators and other unneeded state construction equipment are loaded, as well as agricultural containers that make it possible to grow food on a large scale on the surface of the sea. The ocean liner sails back to the area of operation and remains there as an operations centre, port facility and large-scale power plant until the initial condition is restored. Together with skilled workers who manage the special equipment, the able-bodied locals carry out reconstruction work. The necessary raw materials are obtained from the operation site or imported. The domestic workers who are not able to work, such as children, pregnant women and pensioners, are assigned to agricultural service or household chores. Children are educated by domestic teachers.

6.3.9.3 Evacuation, education, resettlement and reconstruction

All affected citizens are evacuated from the war or disaster area. Ocean liners will be loaded with living containers only. A muster point is expelled at the nearest port or coast where all affected citizens are to assemble. From this point, the ocean liners with the living containers shuttle between the operation site and the home country. All evacuated citizens of the foreign country must be named and approved by their country of origin. Only if the financing of their stay is guaranteed, they are evacuated. Inland, these citizens are treated as asylum seekers and build Asylum Villages[88] . Here they are prepared for actual reconstruction after a disaster, such as the one in their country of origin. Business partnerships and start-ups are also to be discussed, planned and carried out here in the country of origin. As soon as the disaster in the country of origin is over, all citizens are brought back to their country of origin. In their country of origin, they will receive support in the form of machines they brought with them for reconstruction, on which they were trained in the Asylum Village. As soon as the reconstruction is done, all machines have to be delivered back inland in their original condition. The cost of this service varies greatly due to the long period of accommodation. A fixed amount is charged per day in the Asylum Village, which is kept as low as possible because the Asylum Village is mainly self-supporting.

---

88 Ministry of Integration - 8.6.1 Asylum Village

7 People's Protection Service

The People's Protection Service is a security agency that serves several different purposes. It provides standby service for all other security agencies and the Social Service. It is a security service that companies can order and it provides protection squads when citizens request them in a quorum. Mainly, the People's Protection Service provides patrol services for the police, during which it also carries out social missions for the population.

The People's Protection Service can be reached by phone around the clock at 110, on the internet at People's Protection Service.de and on the intranet via the profile page in the Security Directory. Immediate help is available at local police stations, town halls and Social Villages.

7.1 Staff

The People's Protection Service consists of employed security forces from the Ministry of Security and voluntary or affected citizens. The employed security forces are paid monthly and carry out the activity on a full-time basis. Voluntary citizens receive an allowance, the amount of which is determined in the budget vote and must include at least meals.

Employed People's Protection Service are soldiers of the military who have nothing to do at the moment because the defence case has not occurred. These People's Protection Service personnel are the only forces that are transferred to the training bases for a month every year to train new People's Protection Service personnel and also to take part in further training measures themselves. They are also able to use military vehicles and materials for civilian purposes because they are trained in their use. Since the Social Villages become barracks in the event of war, employed People's Protection Officers work closely with the Social Service because they both access military equipment for their services.

People's Protection Service volunteers are citizens who voluntarily sign up for services to accompany other People's Protection Service volunteers. This includes those young adults who have committed to the People's Protection Service for at least three months during their People's Service year. They can also be citizens who are affected by an unsafe situation and want to help improve it through their work with other People's Protection Service members.

7.1.1 Fault

If faults are made in the field, the People's Protection Service officers concerned receive a written reprimand and instructions on how to prevent this fault in the future. If the fault occurs again, a warning is given, and the third time a disciplinary warning with at least one month's leave of absence or transfer. The fourth time is followed by dismissal. Faults that violate the law are dealt with in court proceedings.

7.1.2 Training for the People's Protection Service

Training for service with the People's Protection Service is given to all People's Service workers[89] during their three-month basic training. In the theoretical part, all participants learn which actions on the street are punishable or are to be considered administrative offences. All legal basics for the People's Protection Service are printed on the profile page in the Knowledge Directory, sorted by paragraph, and explained with videos. These basics are tested in the theoretical examinations of the basic training. During the service in the People's Protection Service, this will be the legal basis on which measures are carried out. As soon as you enter that you are a People's Protection Service worker in your profile in the Labour Directory, you will automatically receive a message as soon as paragraphs from the theory lessons of the basic training at that time have been updated.

In the practical lessons, situations are acted out on how to behave as a People's Protection Service in certain situations. From an epileptic fit of a citizen to rioting and looting by several citizens, the most diverse situations are included. Once

---

89 Ministry of Education - 10 People's Service

the situation is under control again, the examinees have to recite the paragraphs that have now authorised them to act in this way.

The wording of the public security and public order paragraphs is issued by the Minister of Security after they have been drafted in a committee. They are binding whenever the People's Protection Service has to use force in an operational service. A warning must be given before the People's Protection Service uses force on its own. Exceptions apply to investigative operations in which a warning would trigger imminent danger. As soon as security forces are attacked, they defend themselves without warning. After a successful use of force, People's Protection Service officers must say on the basis of which paragraphs physical force and direct coercion was used through an arrest.

During their first month on the job, new People's Protection Service officers receive in-service training.

7.1.3 Uniform

The equipment includes uniforms and a belt with tools and weapons. Uniforms are provided for salaried and People's Service providers. Waistcoats are issued for voluntary citizens. The waistcoat is neon yellow with green lettering. On the front it says PEOPLE'S PROTECTION SERVICE and the city coat of arms. On the back it says PEOPLE'S PROTECTION SERVICE, Respect Trust Reason. The armband is neon yellow with black lettering "PEOPLE'S PROTECTION SERVICE". It is worn with the waistcoat and the uniform.

The uniform is green and corresponds to the military's field uniforms. The epaulettes have neon yellow People's Protection Service rank insignia, which vary according to years of service and further training.

7.1.4 Tools

The tools vary according to the patrol service and are usually provided by the security agencies commissioning the People's Protection Service. The following tools are provided as basic necessity for the patrol service. The tools consist of a walkie-talkie, gloves, rubbish bags, cable ties, a multi-function tool with knife and pliers, and a body injury billing device including a wallet. The body injury billing device is used to make criminal or voluntary thugs pay the contribution to the Addictive drugs Health Insurance[90] and issue a receipt with which they can receive treatment. Payment can be made by card or cash. All these tools are not on the belt of every People's Protection Service, but a whole group must have all these tools. On patrol and in the protection squad, People's Protection Service officers also carry non-lethal weapons. Weapons are pepper spray and a remote-combat stun gun. In addition, batons, protective waistcoats and helmets may be worn.

7.1.5 Emergency vehicles

Emergency vehicles are either police or military vehicles used by the People's Protection Service in peacetime. They include cars and trucks for transporting goods and persons. These vehicles are stationed in the Social Villages where they are maintained and used by the Social Service as long as they are not needed for operations. They are retrofitted with removable blue and green lights.

7.2 On-call service for all security agencies and the Social Service

The People's Protection Service can be requested as support by all security agencies. Employed People's Protection Service officers receive further training in all basic areas of responsibility of all security agencies. They take over the briefing of the voluntary People's Protection Service and

---

90Ministry of Health - 5.12.3 Addictive drugs Health Insurance

mediate or accompany them, depending on how many People's Protection Service personnel have been requested. If only a few are requested, voluntary People's Protection Service officers are sent. In addition to the security agencies such as the police, Customs, rescue services, fire brigade or the Technical Relief Agency, the Social Service[91] can also request assistance or hand over tasks. Tasks can be, for example, trips for social commuters, support can be requested for a move to a Social Village, for example. The respective authorities always have the power of command over the People's Protection Service and thus also the democratic responsibility for the operations.

7.3 Security service on order

Private security services are prohibited. Any guarding that is to be enforced by force against persons must be democratically controlled. For this, the People's Protection Service offers a security service that can be deployed anywhere around the clock if it is ordered and paid for. This applies to the protection of objects and persons. Entrepreneurs who want to have their premises guarded by personnel can order the service at any time, for example discotheques or factory premises. Persons who want armed escorts can also order it. The price for the provision costs plus 40% tax of the Planned Economy applies. Availability for commercial use is only allowed for the People's Protection Service if nationals are not neglected as a result. In that case, more staff must be hired.

7.4 Patrol duty for the police including social outreach[92]

The People's Protection Service operational centres are the local police stations. This is where the People's Protection Service meet and get their equipment. The patrol service is primarily there to approve the police so that criminal cases can be solved more often. The People's Protection Service patrols with one police officer, one employed People's Protection Service officer

---

91 Ministry of Planned Economy - 9.4.1 Social Service
92 §10.1 Protection of privacy: BV Art.13, §170.1 Civil courage

and about 3 other voluntary or affected citizens. This team is allowed to split into a maximum of 2 teams but remain in the same patrol area. The team without the policeman can then carry out social missions.

Patrols are carried out either on foot or by bicycle. In a car, the distance to the citizens is too great. The routes for a patrol go through areas where the police have noticed an increased crime rate or areas where many citizens are on foot in public spaces, for example on the street or on forest paths. The people's protection groups are in contact with each other via radio and can reinforce each other.

The tasks of the patrol service mainly include the handling of administrative offences and accidents, but also investigations of robbery, extortion, assault, vandalism and pollution. Particular attention is paid to the target group that has the highest propensity for crime in the crime statistics.

People's Protection Service officers are entitled to control identity cards and, if there is sufficient suspicion, to conduct a search. Searches can be carried out on persons and things carried by these persons. The police officer is always responsible for ordering searches. Use of force must also be ordered or authorised by the police officer during the operation. Provisional arrests are made in case of imminent danger. The offenders are bound with cable ties and handed over to the police as soon as possible.

7.4.1 Social outreach[93]

Social missions are carried out in the patrol service. For this purpose, the patrol team splits up for a short time. Police officers always remain in the part of the team that continues the patrol duty. The others split off, provide assistance for a short time and then rejoin the team.

---

93 §9,2 Right to assistance in emergency situations: BV Art.12

7.4.1.1 Help in human emergencies

The People's Protection Service is there for all citizens who lack the short-term help of a family or circle of friends. The Social Emergency Service[94] is responsible for social welfare and can be contacted by the People's Protection Service on request. Anyone who needs short-term help can report to the People's Protection Service by telephone, digitally or in person. Voluntary People's Protection Service officers from the nearest patrol visit the person in need and help. For example, someone cannot move or manage things on their own that a large family or group of friends could otherwise do together at short notice. Such things are managed by lone domestic nationals together with the People's Protection Service. As a report to the person in need of help, the People's Protection Service should say, "Reinforcements have arrived! How can we help?"

The rest of the team continues the patrol duty. After the assistance has been rendered, the two groups of the team come together again by radio. If they find that the help was requested because the person was lonely, they invite the person to go for a walk. The walk consists of accompanying the People's Protection Service on their patrol.

7.4.1.2 Help in emergencies of nature

While on patrol, at least one People's Protection Service member of the group must carry a rubbish bag and gloves to pick up litter that is lying around. The bin liner is then emptied into the nearest public bin. The People's Protection Service is supposed to protect humans and the environment. Collecting rubbish is part of the job for all People's Protection Services when they are on duty.

94Ministry of Planned Economy - 17.2 Social Emergency Call

7.4.2 Protection squad

The protection squad can be requested by citizens from the age of 10 at the town hall or via the People's Computer. This becomes necessary whenever many citizens in one place feel unsafe, for example, threatened by violent attacks or by series of burglaries in the neighbourhood.

As soon as a quorum of 40% of the affected population within a radius of 0.5 kilometres is reached, the protection squad is dispatched. The higher the number of affected citizens per square kilometre, the smaller the radius may be.

On the People's Protection Service profile page there is a button that says "Request protection squad". Now you can specify a time or period and set a point on the map from which a circle is drawn marking the area of operation. As soon as there are already requirements in this area that overlap, the requirement is added to the quorum. Users can see how many persons have already participated and which area is specifically involved.

Once the quorum is met, the area will be patrolled for 6 months at different times, but mainly at the times indicated by the affected citizens.

The protection squad consists of 12 persons. 2 police officers, 2 employed People's Protection Service officers and 8 voluntary People's Protection Service officers, who are local citizens if possible. The 12 persons are divided into different shifts, some of them wearing civilian clothes. Each shift must be accompanied by at least one police officer or employed People's Protection Service officer. The protection squad always performs a patrol duty and is therefore under the overall command of the police.

7.5 Awards

For People's Protection Service, there is a medal for anyone who has been there for 5 years without receiving a disciplinary warning. There are decorations for special services to humanity and welfare, which are also awarded to helpers with civil courage.

7.6 Dispute resolution

The People's Protection Service often intervenes in conflict situations in its service. However, it also specifically helps to avoid them in advance and offers secured rooms for verbal or physical violence for this purpose. Either parties to the conflict are taken to the special premises by means of brief arrests, or the citizens themselves are allowed to register violent actions and carry them out in a place that the People's Protection Service secures so that no bystanders are harmed. All participants must agree to engage in violence. Otherwise, the People's Protection Service uses the following special mediation tools.

7.6.1 Conciliation cells

A small ISO container is equipped with two cells separated by an armoured glass pane. Slits in the glass allow them to talk to the other side. Two disputing parties are locked up there by the People's Protection Service or the police until they have settled their dispute. This may not last longer than 2 hours. The container can be set up in public if too many people are arguing. Otherwise, the cells can also be built into the police station. If a dispute has public significance, i.e. if many persons are affected by it, the container is set up at a public festival, for example, so that disputants can reconcile there. If politicians are arguing, this dispute can be broadcast on Government Television.

7.6.2 Duel

If two disputants want to fight or brawl, they must do so in a designated area and wear high-visibility waistcoats. Both parties must pay money into the Addictive drugs Health Insurance, which covers bodily injuries after fights, and get a receipt. Provided a duel is orderly and both parties agree to this form of dispute resolution, everything is legal. However, anyone who does not fight in a designated zone or there without a high-visibility waistcoat will at the very least be convicted of causing a public nuisance and bodily harm. The zones in which one is allowed to duel are expelled by the local police and secured by the People's Protection Service. So you have to go to the police or People's Protection Service before you fight to ask where you are allowed to fight. The People's Protection Service then cordons off and secures this area.

7.6.3 Brawl

If many humans want to gather to beat or otherwise fight because they enjoy it and do it expressly on a voluntary basis, they may register a brawl with the police. Sports arenas can also be hired for brawls. Specially signposted brawl arenas can be used at any time to fight without having to report this to the police beforehand. These arenas must be supervised by at least one People's Protection Service officer equipped with a body injury billing device and a purse. Before each fight, both parties must also pay into the Addictive drugs Health Insurance. In return, they receive a receipt which they can use to have the injuries treated by the physician. This receipt is also deposited on the Health Card at the same time so that the treatment can be billed via the Health Card. Injuries must not be older than the receipt, but must be just as old. If in doubt, a photo of the injury should be taken with the People's Protection Service's walkie-talkie after the fight. The People's Protection Service is always a witness and has seen both persons before when settling the Addictive drugs Health Insurance contribution.

8 Police[95]

The Ministry of Security regulates how the police establish public security in the Police Act. This includes principles and laws under which the police operate and how they are organised and run. In particular, the police are responsible for law enforcement and the enforcement of maritime security, aviation security and road traffic law. The police are

---

95§169,6 Safety, §70,2 Supervision: BV Art.169, §71,4 Review of effectiveness

subdivided into the riot police, the civil police, digital police and the constitutional protection as an audit service. The riot police are responsible for patrol duties in cooperation with the People's Protection Service. The Civil Police investigate criminals, bring them to the responsible courts and cooperate with the responsible public prosecutor's office.[96] The digital police do the same on the internet and intranet. The Office for the Protection of the Constitution conducts preliminary investigations in state agencies and cooperates with the Company Auditing Agency and other audit services for the control of state bodies.

All municipalities have at least one police station, for which the deputy minister of security of the municipality is responsible. The Minister of Security ensures nationwide cooperation between all police stations and, in voting with the Ministry of Foreign Affairs, facilitates cross-border law enforcement by foreign police services.

In order to carry out searches or surveillance on persons suspected of having committed a crime, the police must ask the responsible public prosecutor's office for permission. If a case is not cleared up by its statute of limitations, it is closed. Cases that are cleared up are handed over to the public prosecutor's office to initiate court proceedings.

8.1 Equipment

The equipment of the police is used to deploy command and control means with up-to-date technology and the appropriate logistics. Police officers carry cameras, weapons, handcuffs, torches, multifunctional tools, gloves and rubbish bags as tools. Every police officer is equipped with a body camera with an integrated microphone on the shoulder and a tracking device that records location and altitude. Police officers on dangerous special missions also wear a helmet with an integrated 360° 3D camera and bulletproof clothing. The camera equipment is used to keep digital police records and to ensure transparency in the service of the security forces.

Police officers are not equipped with lethal firearms, but with

96Ministry of Justice - 5.6.3 Public Prosecutor's Office

non-lethal firearms for close and long range combat, which they may use in the event of violence or escape attempts. In the case of verbal violence, the use of the weapon must be announced. For example, if a person insults a police officer, the police officer asks the person to stop or the weapon will be used. If the person does not comply, the police officer will inflict slight bodily harm without further warning, for example by spraying pepper spray into the eyes.

8.2 Emergency vehicles

Police officers go on missions in a car equipped with blue lights, loudspeakers and sirens. In each police vehicle there are helmets, protective waistcoats, batons and a drone. Cameras with directional microphones are mounted on the roof in the blue light, which record the three-dimensional all-round view and are recorded in the digital police files and service reports. Most emergency vehicles have 4 or 8 seats, of which at least 2 seats are suitable for arrestees.

For other special missions, there are specially equipped vehicles, such as mobile operations centres, mobile custody cells, water cannons, armoured cars or public address vehicles, police helicopters or similar aircraft and drones.

8.3 Digital police files[97]

The police information system runs via radio, the Security Directory and the Investigation Directory. In order to be able to identify persons quickly, the police have continuous access to the registration system from the Persons Directory and the Residents' Registration Office[98] . All information is stored in digital police files, which are kept in the Investigation Directory for prosecution and in the Security Directory for assistance. For data protection in the security sector, it is necessary to protect data for investigative tactical reasons in such a way that they can be kept secret. For international and European

---

[97] §10 Protection of privacy: BV Art.13, §169,4 Security
[98] Ministry of Integration - 4.4 Residents' Registration Office

cooperation, the necessary data is shared with EUROPOL if the Minister of Security grants data release in individual cases or across the board.

Police officers are responsible for keeping digital police records. The video data from all cameras is sent in real time via radio to the servers of the Ministry of Security and stored in the Security Directory. At the end of a shift, the police officer has to review the videos of his shift in his closed group in the Security Directory. The programme immediately transcribes all the audio recordings present in the videos. Each police officer reads through the automatically generated texts and corrects any faults. Manipulation is punishable by law and can be traced on the original sound and the automatic translation. His movement profile is displayed in the virtual inland[99], which also includes all indoor areas. This data comes from satellite photos and from the Real Estate Directory[100], which records all buildings including rooms. This documents all actions of all police officers.

Criminological services, such as recording and prosecuting reports, are filed in cases, which are given their own profiles in the Investigation Directory. Everything that belongs to a case is marked in the video or in the text of the respective shift by the police officer in terms of time or paragraph. No matter which working method, text or video editing, the police officer decides on, the programme transfers the information to the video or text at the same time. In one case, notices, searches, warrants, expulsions, administrative offences and criminal offences can be created as files by the police officer, which must be automatically filled in and controlled by the police officer. Matching laws and paragraphs are automatically linked and controlled by the police officer or the public prosecutor's office.

For example, there was a theft. The police filmed the crime scene, interrogated the victims and videotaped the complaint from the complainant. At the end of the shift, the police officer creates a report. First, he has to select the time during his shift when he was investigating the case. Now the programme

---

99 Ministry of Digital Affairs - 11.4.3.5 Central: Playing Field
100 Ministry of Infrastructure - 4.5 Real Estate Directory

immediately enters the profiles of the persons from the Persons Directory into the form for the report via facial recognition on the video and all statements from the police officer's video log are immediately assigned to the matching person. The police officer must now specify who is the victim, offender or witness. If the offender is unknown, a phantom profile is created. For this purpose, witnesses or victims are given a computer with a programme for phantom pictures and fields to indicate age, sex, place of action and time of the crime. The data of all witnesses and police officers involved are entered into the profile of the case in the Investigation Directory. An algorithm automatically identifies all possible offenders. The police officer can assess the witness statements as credible or implausible and enter this via a slider in the programme to influence the result of the overall search.

8.4 Investigation Directory[101]

The Investigation Directory consists of profiles of cases. Persons who are being searched for are described as precisely as possible in the profile of the case. For this purpose, all data of the intranet and internet about this person are listed. The data can be supplemented by the investigators and, if necessary, also by freelance investigators. In one case, the profiles of victims, offenders and witnesses from the Persons Directory and the profiles of Ministry of Security workers from the Labour Directory are brought together and related to the case. If companies are victims or offenders, their profiles from the Labour Directory are added to the case. All security agencies and judicial officers investigating a case form a search group for that case.

As long as a case is being investigated and solved, it is secret. Publication takes place as soon as the case is closed or a legally binding verdict has been reached. Investigative tactics can be made unrecognisable for publication. The Investigation Directory is accessible without restriction only to the police and the responsible public prosecutor's office. Cases are transferred to the Court Directory as soon as cases involving

---

101 §169.4 Security

police investigations are heard in court proceedings.

The Investigation Directory is the central collection point for criminal offences and misdemeanours of all kinds. It is also a digital database so that the Security and Ministry of Justice can access the files of all cases. This database is shared with all states, which also share their criminal cases, convicted criminals and wanted lists with the Ministry of Security. The Investigation Directory is to be shared, if possible, by all European Union Member States from the Schengen area for registration on wanted persons.

8.4.1 Open search groups

Certain cases and facts can be put out for free search by an investigation team in voting with the deputy minister of security. Voluntary citizens can register as free investigators in the Investigation Directory. Steps taken must be documented and categorised so that the police can link and coordinate them with other investigators. Freelance investigators can also receive targeted search assignments from investigators. However, the police must not inform the other freelance investigators about this in order not to jeopardise the manhunt. The police have an overview of all investigators inland, the investigators themselves do not.

With the free search, users can view all persons for whom an alert has been issued and digitally compare whether there is a connection to the suspect who is wanted on a warrant and how much the reward is. Citizens now have the possibility of being shown persons from their circle of acquaintances who could be connected to the wanted person. For this digital comparison of data, the free investigator must allow access to all his data so that the free investigator's personal network can be examined for contacts in his circle of acquaintances. The freelance investigators then try to find clues or informants to determine the whereabouts of the wanted person. They are shown crime scenes and reported places of residence or whereabouts of the wanted person, which the investigators have released. The simulation via the virtual map[102] serves

---

102 Ministry of Digital Affairs - 11.4.3.5 Central: Playing Field

to simplify the presentation of persons connecting to the suspected offender.

If there is urgent information, a direct message can be sent to investigators with a reference to the free investigator's search report and where the urgent information can be found in it. If the free investigator is in the real world outside the Investigation Directory, he can alert the police directly and pass on his information. Steps that could endanger the free investigator are only permissible after consultation with and approval by the police.

8.5 Civil police

The civil police are responsible for investigating criminal cases in civil and criminal law. Their staff do not wear uniforms while on service and also investigate undercover. The civil police do not go on patrol, but investigate criminals who are unknown or on the run. Operations that involve violence or immediate coercion through arrest are supposed to be carried out with uniformed police officers because they wear surveillance cameras, names and service numbers on their uniforms. Only if there is imminent danger may plainclothes police officers immediately overpower and arrest the fleeing offender.

The civil police are used for all suspected criminal offences. As soon as sufficient evidence has been gathered for a prosecution, the public prosecutor's office takes over the case and transfers it to court proceedings. The public prosecutor's office decides whether the evidence is sufficient.

The civilian police need extensive expertise for their searches. The search areas are so extensive in themselves that specialists are needed. These specialists are sorted by ministry and work in the capital city of the Ministry of Security. They support the civilian police officers in the field with specialist knowledge from a distance. For more extensive special investigations, specialists can be sent to the responsible police station and live on site for the duration of the special investigation.

8.5.1 Civil police operations

Civil police operations arise from reports from citizens or ministries. In these reports, the suspicion is sufficient to send a civilian patrol. Since there is no regular patrol service in the civilian police, more personnel can be sent for undercover investigations in case of suspicious reports. Civilian police patrol public places, companies, research institutions or families when reports are received. In order to infiltrate undercover investigators, the falsification of degrees and CVs is permissible for the undercover investigators.

For example, in the public sphere, these would be gangs that control certain streets in order to engage in illegal trade, extort protection money or carry out other crimes. They could be reported to the police by alert or affected citizens. Here, the civil police would post an observation patrol in this public space at the reported focus times.

In companies, superiors could cover up the behaviour of an employee who treats other employees unfairly in the line of duty, e.g. promises a pay rise, promotion or transfer and does not keep it or does not apply the same conditions to other employees. For example, a report could be made to the police by affected staff, customers or residents. The civil police would bring in an employee, provider or customer to verify the report.

In research institutions, employees might do authoritative research work for superiors but not be mentioned. The mention in the publications, i.e. the authors' list, must be placed according to working hours and workload. For example, the first author cannot be a professor who has only had staff do research at his or her department. Here, students, research assistants, other laboratory staff or doctoral students could make a report to the local police station. The civilian police would, for example, sneak a doctoral student into the research institution to document the unjust behaviour.

In families, children or parents could cover up for, promote or carry out the misconduct against a family member. Here, for example, an observing parent, friend or relative of any age could make a report to the police. The civilian police will now infiltrate the family's circle of friends with an undercover investigator and observe the incidents or provide the affected persons with the means for video surveillance.

8.5.2 Undercover investigations

In all undercover investigations, the plainclothes police officers will never make arrests themselves to protect their identity, but the uniformed police will do so if possible. Undercover investigators will stay on the case a little longer and observe whether there is an improvement and leave the investigation area again as unnoticed as possible. Sometimes this will result in a simulated arrest of the undercover investigators, sometimes in a period of leave-taking or termination lasting weeks.

The names of undercover investigators are given with pseudonyms in the court records and access logs from the intranet and are changed into the real plain names after their death. If, for reasons of identity protection of a civilian police officer, it is also necessary to keep his or her acts of evidence preservation secret, these facts must also be published after his or her death. Actions to preserve evidence can be kept secret for tactical investigative reasons if this would permanently expose the investigative tactics of the civilian police officers and new working methods would have to be developed.

8.6 Special task force

As soon as criminals have lethal firearms, the special task force is appointed. It consists of soldiers who have received the best possible training in handling lethal weapons. Special task forces for rapid deployment are available in the municipalities. People's Protection Service soldiers and police officers arm themselves with lethal weapons and bulletproof shields, waistcoats and helmets at the police station.

In the case of hostage-taking, the national special task force is appointed. It consists of military special forces who are trained to act as unnoticed as possible.

8.7 Digital police

The police are not only present on the streets, but also on the internet and intranet. The citizens who move in the digital world should feel just as safe there as they do in the real world. In the digital world, the digital police ensure that users can report crimes so that these crimes can be solved, deleted and those responsible brought before a court.

It is responsible for the prosecution of crimes committed with the help of information and communication technology. The police's cyber capabilities are ensured by equipping them with up-to-date hardware and software from the People's Innovation Company Intranet. In addition, the digital police work with the military's digital warfare security forces and are assisted in cyber defence and programming of new digital tools and weapons by the Institute for Information Security.[103] In the event of cyber attacks, the police identify the offenders and carry out counter-attacks with the military's obsolete cyber weapons.

8.7.1 Internet

On the internet, site operators are obliged to keep the content of their sites free of criminal offences or, in case of doubt, to report criminal offences to the police. Criminal foreign content will be deleted, domestic authors will be reported and brought before a court by the digital police. Just as owners of restaurants ensure the safety of their guests and alert the police in case of violations, operators of internet platforms do the same. Users of the internet can also send the internet address directly to the police at any time or forward the email if they discover a suspected offence. In this way, users search the internet and report crimes they observe there. The population can report observed suspected crimes to the police through digital policing, just like in real life. At www.police.online, the internet address where the alleged crime was committed can be inserted. Suspected criminal emails can be forwarded to

---

103 Ministry of Digital Affairs - 8 Digital Crime, 13 People's Innovation Company Intranet

the address crime@police.online. If the offence is committed within the framework of an app, the user must go to the police website with his smartphone and allow access to his smartphone. Then he can access the app via the website in his smartphone and show the offence. The entire image and sound content of the smartphone is automatically recorded and sent to the police. A plug-in for browsers or an app for the smartphone can also be downloaded from www.police. online, with which the police recording can be switched on immediately during the page visit. The internet address, page history, all trackers and cookies are automatically saved until the recording is switched off by the user. Afterwards, the user must enter information in a hearing form.

The police then determine the IP address of the computer or smartphone and contact the accused. Either operators delete a post within 24 hours or their website is blocked inland until the criminal content has been deleted. If a website only serves to make criminal content accessible, the entire site is immediately blocked inland. If it is located on servers inland, the affected data will be deleted or the servers will be confiscated and court proceedings opened. Accused persons have the right to consult a lawyer at any time and to open court proceedings against the digital police by filing an objection in order to defend themselves against the above-mentioned digital coercive measures.

8.7.2 Intranet

In the People's Navigator[104] for the intranet, the police plug-in for the Internet is already pre-installed. Here, however, it is possible to directly click on persons who are responsible for replies, comments, posts, groups, profiles or pages. These names are either in the header of a news and profile or in the imprint of a group or page. The names are linked directly to the matching profile of the responsible person in the Persons Directory. The accused can be included here directly by the user. The input fields to be filled in after a police report are already the fields to be filled in for a new case in the

104 Ministry of Digital Affairs - 11.4 People's Navigator

Investigation Directory. People's Computer users can open a new case immediately by filing a report. As soon as the police audits the case, a new profile is created in the Investigation Directory.

For all privately operated intranet sites, the same measures apply as for internet site operators. On the intranet, however, the assignment for each content to a People's Computer and thus also to an identity card is possible, which reduces the investigation effort.

The police, in cooperation with international election observers, verify the People's Computer voting. This work is done on a random basis and under the direction of the international election observers. The Department for Constitutional Protection in the Digital Police is responsible for ensuring that international election observers also comply with domestic data protection laws, but also for immediate tracing in the event of suspected election fraud.

8.7.3 Data retrieval

The police are the only agency authorised to secretly retrieve all personal data from all People's Computers. Such secret retrieval is not shown in the access log[105] until the proceedings in court are completed. All other security forces require prior clearance from the Ministry of Justice. The police must immediately report any secret data retrieval to the responsible prosecutor's office and create an access log on the profile of the case in the Investigation Directory. Once the case has been closed, the accesses must be recorded in the Access Directory.

8.8 Crime

The People's Protection Service, the police and the military are responsible for crime prevention, partly in cooperation with the authorities of the Ministries of Justice and Digital Affairs. Light crime is recorded by the patrol service of the People's Protection Service and usually punished directly

---

105 Ministry of Digital Affairs - 7.5 Access Directory

with measures against misdemeanours. Serious and organised crime is dealt with by the police, if necessary using additional military security forces, and brought to justice in cooperation with the responsible public prosecutor's office. The civilian police or digital police are responsible for real or digital economic and sabotage protection and counterintelligence. In cooperation with the military, the civil police conduct investigations into NBC crime, i.e. when nuclear, biological or chemical warfare agents are to be produced or used. The Office for the Protection of the Constitution is responsible for any crime committed by the state or on its orders.

8.9 Institute for Criminology

The Institute of Criminology continuously researches reasons and personality profiles for light, serious and organised crime inland. From this, it develops measures for crime prevention, law enforcement, counterintelligence, economic protection and sabotage protection. New measures are developed and tested in cooperation with investigators. Successful measures are shared with all investigators in a catalogue of measures.

8.10 Riot[106]

Rioting is a punishable action carried out by or from a group of individuals, but subsequently covered up by the group. Such punishable actions include damage to property, looting, pillaging, ambushes, assault and attacks on security forces. Rioting based on a group's need for prestige is considered a precursor to civil war. Rioting based on political beliefs is considered a precursor to revolt.

Rioters seeking validity are given the opportunity to solve their socio-psychological problems through compromise or exclusion. Committees determine whether the rest of the citizens and the rioters can eliminate the cause in joint laws or whether rioters should withdraw into a cultural protection

---

106§173,2 Army: BV Art.58, §172,2c Internal and external security in a state of emergency

area where they can eliminate the cause with their own laws. Rioters who have a psychologically stressful past receive psychological care and, if desired, a change of milieu. Similar to the witness protection programme, they can relocate to a Social Village or a Barter Economy Zone to find new friends and colleagues.

Humans are not blind even in a crowd, they have reasons for their actions, especially when they do it as a group. There must be a unified image of the enemy in the group where it is permissible to carry out punishable actions, which is otherwise absent among the group members themselves. This is the starting point. The image of the enemy must be explored. It is the task of the politicians to find out the reasons for the discomfort of their citizens and to eliminate them. If they cannot do this alone, they consult the citizens in a committee.

8.10.1 Police intervention during riots

In the event of rioting, a state of emergency must be declared by the Minister of Security in voting with the Minister of State Organisation.[107] The police lead the operation, the People's Protection Service and the military support with personnel and equipment. In the event of riots, it is important to surround the area as completely as possible in order to be able to apprehend all the persons involved. Surveillance from the air, which is as complete as possible, creates movement profiles of the groups and individual members. As soon as foreigners have travelled into the inland for the riot and then want to flee again, the national external borders are controlled by Customs.

Helicopters circle over the area of operation, police helicopters monitor the area and are supported by military combat helicopters equipped for terrain reconnaissance and loaded with irritant gas or sleeping gas in their guns.

The police first make the announcement to stop the rioting immediately and to surrender to the police with their hands up. Rioters who do not do so are rounded up with water

---

107 Ministry of State Organisation - 12.7 State of emergency, 12.4 Protests, 12.7.4 Civil war, 12.7.5 Revolt

cannons and police armoured clearing vehicles and numbed with irritant gas or sleeping gas. The security forces then enter the crowd with gas masks and handcuffs and arrest all persons. If too many rioters are wearing gas masks, networks are thrown out by drones and all participants are arrested at the edges. All those arrested are remanded in custody at the nearest prison until the court proceedings are completed. While still in custody, detainees should write down the reasons for their actions and forward them to the External Service of the Federal Moderator's Office[108] . Rioters must pay damages and face imprisonment.[109]

After riots, nationals must be discouraged from participating in the future. On the one hand, this is done through a political solution if the riots are politically motivated. On the other hand, the domestic rioters are sent to detention and are rehabilitated there. The resocialisation programme takes place in the solitary cell and is a predetermined plan on civics from the Knowledge Directory with a final exam.

Foreigners are deported or expelled after participating in riots, depending on whether they live inland or entered for the riot. They are banned from entering the country for life.

8.11 Fighting the Mafia

Organised crime derives its assets mainly from the trade in drugs, weapons, forced prostitution, human trafficking and extortion. The means of livelihood are being withdrawn. The trade in drugs will be legalised and audited, as will prostitution and immigration. Lethal weapons may now only be sold and stored in police stations. Blackmail will be immediately documented. For this purpose, spying devices are issued to victims. If suspicions are confirmed, undercover investigators are assigned to pursue the offenders and identify those behind them.

Once the gang is detained at the same time, victims are placed in the witness protection programme if they so wish. Victims in the witness protection programme are replaced at their

108 Ministry of State Organisation - 4.4.2 External Service
109 Ministry of Justice - 8.13.7 Rioting

place of residence and work by undercover investigators. If revenge is taken by the mafia, the avengers and their backers are identified.[110] Any property belonging to the criminal organisation and any assets of the detainees are confiscated. In the case of foreign criminal organisations, visa-free travel may be restricted, entry bans imposed, cooperation with foreign security agencies increased or travel and trade relations interrupted if the affected state does not cooperate.

The European secret service is responsible for tracking down, spying on and kidnapping mafia bosses all over the world so that they can be brought to justice or killed if necessary.

8.12 City raid[111]

As soon as the crime rate exceeds the mark of 10 000 crimes per 100 000 inhabitants in a year, a city raid is carried out. The responsibility for its proper implementation lies with the Minister of Security and not the deputy of the affected municipality. A city raid is considered a state of emergency in which many bystanders are affected. At the same time, there are always many confidants who know about the offences and condone them instead of reporting them. Therefore, this unpleasant state of affairs is also due to the complicity of many citizens of the city.

8.12.1 Rule of law observation

During the city raid, many civil rights are suspended locally and temporarily. Observers from the United Nations[112] , camera teams from the Ministry of Media Affairs and judges from the Ministry of Justice are deployed to monitor the situation to ensure that there is no arbitrary or unnecessary violence by the security forces. The observers enter through the city limits where they are controlled by Customs. Observers stay among the civilian population in civilian clothes, can go anywhere

---

110 Ministry of Justice - 8.13.4 Organised crime
111 §173,2 Army: BV Art. 58, §172,2b Internal and external security in a state of emergency
112 https://www.un.org/en/

through their observer pass, are let through everywhere, are allowed to document everything and get an answer to all their questions from the security forces.

8.12.2 Monitoring

Police helicopters as well as reconnaissance helicopters and drones from the military monitor and document the city from the air throughout the entire period. These recordings are used to coordinate the forces, secure the border and may later become important evidence.

8.12.3 Lockdown

The military and Customs secure the entire land and water border area of the city. How the control border runs is decided by the police. Criminal statistics investigations can be used to find out which suburbs support the city with criminal energy. These suburbs are included in the city raid.
A city raid may last for a maximum of 3 days. During this time, the city is sealed off by a large contingent of security forces. Nothing and no one can get in or out.
The mobile network, telephone and internet are switched off and jammers are set up. Only the intranet remains active. All public and private local and long-distance transport is shut down.

8.12.4 Special squad

In each neighbourhood there is a special squad for persons who refuse to leave immediately. It consists of 10 People's Protection Service officers and one police officer. Anyone who resists the city raid is immediately detained for the duration of the city raid. A mobile prison is set up in the city for detentions.
In case of armed resistance, a national special task force arrives and clears the building by force of arms if necessary. In the event of a hostage situation, the hostage-takers are cleared for

shooting. However, the lives of the hostages have top priority. If it is possible to free the hostages by killing the hostage-takers, this option should be chosen. For this purpose, snipers, gases or poisons of the military are used.

8.12.5 Uprising riots

As soon as there are riots, heavy tanks and attack helicopters are deployed to this part of the city. The attack helicopters are equipped with sleeping gas, tear gas and a super-heavy machine gun that can shoot through walls. The Leopard 2 A5 tanks are loaded with ammunition so that the big gun can fire shells containing tear gas, sleeping gas, networks or coloured water, which are fired over the heads of a crowd of people, where they explode and release the gas or coloured water. The coloured water is used to mark everyone involved in the riot. The tank also has smoke cannons, also armed with tear gas and sleeping gas, to disperse insurgents around the tank. On top of the turret is a remote-controlled machine gun with rubber bullets.
Lethal firearms are used by the military and the police as soon as firearms are used by persons, even if only dummies for deterrence. As soon as security forces are threatened with a weapon that looks like a lethal firearm, these persons may be engaged with lethal firearms. Likewise, vehicles may be fired upon to stop them.

8.12.6 Commuter

Workers or travellers returning to the city get an exemption permit at the border post on the outskirts of the city to move with their vehicle to their place of residence. Start and destination addresses are entered in the exemption permit. Commuters from foreign cities are controlled at the city border checkpoint and are then allowed to leave the city. All returning travellers and returning commuters who were travelling by public transport will be taken to their place of residence by police buses. The police buses that transported police officers from all over the country to the city raid are used for this purpose.

8.12.7 Procedure

The night before, security forces from all over the country set out for the city raid. Only the command knows where the journey is going. The drivers move to specific waypoints and are told where to go next. About 30km before they reach their destination, they are given their exact address where they will be deployed in the city.

8.12.7.1 Demarcation

The military is responsible for all perimeter security around the city. Some access roads are manned by Customs with checkpoints. Other access roads are closed off by the military and manned with guards. Vehicles that try to break through the cordon are stopped with firearms. The entire border area around the city is covered with barbed wire and patrolled by all-terrain vehicles or light tanks. All soldiers securing this border carry firearms. Crossing the border outside the checkpoints is considered a criminal offence and is punished with a warning cry of "Stop or I will shoot! If the offender does not stop within 2 seconds, his feet and lower legs are shot at to prevent him from escaping.
Customs controls every vehicle at the city border checkpoints without exception, except for entering security forces vehicles, they only have to show the service cards of all occupants.
As soon as the border is secured, a disaster alarm is triggered and the surrounding forces of prevention of danger are alerted. Surveillance Television[113] is now also alerted and has to send many monitoring teams into the city. There are special emergency plans for this, which are coordinated with all the authorities and broadcasters involved and take effect in the event of a disaster.

---

113 Ministry of Media - 12 Surveillance Television

8.12.7.2 Structure

The military arrives with trucks, personnel carriers, light and heavy tanks, drones and helicopters. They are taking up positions around the city, establishing a base in the city centre and setting up control tents and living tents with the residents in all neighbourhoods at designated locations.
In the city centre, the military sets up a base for senior police officers, ministers and members of the press. The military occupies a specially secured corridor for this purpose, through which the politicians and journalists are escorted to the base. While the security forces take the persons out of the houses, soldiers set up control tents in the neighbourhoods.

8.12.7.3 Search

While the military and Customs set up border protection, the police with the People's Protection Service and the residual forces of the military and Customs advance into the city from all sides. The first cars of the column drive into the city centre with blue lights. From there, a backlog of security forces forms in their patrol cars. Each emergency vehicle has a house number that it must head for.
Buildings are surrounded by soldiers, People's Protection Service and customs officers and police officers take all persons out of the house. One policeman is placed per flat so that all residents are taken out of their houses and workers from the companies as simultaneously as possible. Locked doors are broken down. The policeman is armed with non-lethal weapons and a bulletproof shield. He searches the home or company for persons only. He instructs all persons to leave the building immediately through the main exit. Persons are only allowed to wear clothes on their body, take their identity card, children or pets with them. The police officer makes sure that everyone leaves the location and leaves the entrance door open when leaving so that it does not have to be broken open for the search. As soon as there are no more persons in a house, all the police officers start searching one room after the other together. They are accompanied by sniffer dogs from

the police, military or Customs. After the search, the entrance door is closed and sealed with a green tape. If a criminal object is found during the search, the entrance door is sealed and newly examined by the forensic team.

Without exception, all properties are searched, whether private residences or company buildings. Locked doors are forced open if the owner cannot be found. Hidden weapons, stolen goods, burglary tools, crime tools, criminals or victims are searched for. Each house search is monitored with 360° cameras set up in the home. The police officers also wear their body cameras. After the city raid, residents can download and view the video of their search on their People's Computer. Theft or damage can be reported to the prosecutor's office in the local court with this evidence. Damaged or lost permissible goods that are not evidence of a crime will be replaced.

8.12.7.4 Accommodation

In front of the house, other security forces receive the residents or workers and explain to them that they are experiencing a city raid, what their rights and duties are now, what the procedure is, what to do next and when it will all be over. The security forces that previously surrounded the house now surround the humans from the houses. One security force guards the admission to each house.

All persons have to line up on the street and wait for the disaster management. As soon as the disaster management arrives, tents and containers are set up together with the residents, just as it happens in the case of a natural disaster. This is not only an exercise for the disaster management staff, but also for the persons who witness it.

The shelters consist of tents and containers that residents set up together with their neighbours in front of their homes under the guidance of a disaster management worker. It is already determined in advance whose flat search will be carried out last. These persons are accommodated in more comfortable containers.

8.12.7.5 People check

All persons who are in the city at the time of the city raid must report to different stations in the control tent of their neighbourhood after leaving their home or company.

At the first station are People's Protection Service officers who control the identity cards and, if necessary, profile the person on the Persons Directory Intranet so that all the data collected is stored there. At the second station, DNA samples are taken from all citizens, compared with the currently unsolved criminal cases and then destroyed.

At the third station in the control tent, each person is examined individually and unclothed by a physician. If injuries are discovered, the physician photographs the patient and his injuries with his People's Computer and sends him to the police for questioning. Here he has to state where the injuries came from. The physician is bound by confidentiality and each person is alone in the room with the physician. Anyone who has been a victim or witness of a crime that has not been reported so far can request a report here without being noticed. To do so, one must have one's identity card photographed by the physician. The personal data of the identity card and, if applicable, the photos of injuries, are transmitted to the police.

Only those who have been victims of or witnesses to a crime or are criminals and wish to turn themselves in to the police go to the fourth station. Police officers interview the persons and open cases or assign them to existing cases.

As soon as you have been controlled by the police and medically examined in the control tent, you wait again in your accommodation until your own flat has been searched. If nothing is found, you are allowed back into your flat. If something is found, the flat is sealed. All residents of the affected house are immediately detained and only interrogated after the city raid, because all available security forces are needed.

8.12.7.6 Living conditions

There is a curfew throughout the city raid. Anyone with a concern must walk and report to their neighbourhood control tent. From there, sick people are taken away and food is distributed. Emergencies are taken to the nearest hospital, and suspects who fall ill are taken to the nearest detention hospital. Disaster management supports the control tents with food. This food comes from all supermarkets in the city, which are perishable quickly, and additionally from food rations from the disaster management warehouse, which will soon reach the expiry date.

8.12.8 Follow-up

After the city raid, there will be more People's Motor Vehicle Government Television visits with citizens' committees in the neighbourhoods that were heavily affected by crime in the next 4 weeks. After one year, the balance sheet from the city raid will be drawn. Unless the crime rate has dropped below 10 000 crimes per 100 000 inhabitants, the citizens of the city and the neighbourhoods will be asked if they want to live in such an unsafe city. If they vote in favour, it will be noted on the town entrance signs. If the citizens decide against it, the rights of freedom in the city are restricted until the desired security enters. How far to go here is always decided at each step by the citizens of the city or neighbourhood affected.

9 Customs[114]

Customs is responsible for the entry and departure of persons and for the import and export of goods and services. Together with the Customs Investigation and Tax Investigation Departments, it is responsible for controls, inspections and enforcement under Customs, criminal and administrative offences law.

Customs shall provide and receive administrative and legal assistance to other security agencies and ministries as notified. Customs shall cooperate with other security forces

---

114§152,1,2 Tariffs: BV Art.133

and ministries. The other security forces may be requested by Customs to assist in order to be able to use material and personnel at short notice.

Customs controls the entry and departure of all persons as well as the imports and exports of all goods into and from the inland at the border posts. Customs collects tariffs on imports and exports there, or digitally in the case of advance notification.

The tax code for tariffs is issued by the Ministry of Foreign Affairs, that for taxes is issued by the Ministry of Finance, and the Ministries of Labour and Economic Affairs may provide for further levies. Taxes from defaulting tax evaders or undeclared workers are managed by the Tax Investigation Department.

Bans and restrictions on the entry or departure of persons, are issued by the Ministry of Integration or a court judgment. The import or export of goods and services may be prohibited or restricted by the ministries of Foreign Affairs, Health, Labour and Economic Affairs. The Ministries of Economy may determine further regularisations in foreign trade and market regulation law and have them controlled and enforced by Customs.

9.1 Cooperation with other ministries

Customs regularly cooperates with the ministries of Foreign Affairs, Integration, Health, Finance, Labour, Justice and Economic Affairs.

The Ministry of Foreign Affairs informs Customs which foreigners are allowed to enter the inland and for how long.[115]

Customs informs the Ministry of Foreign Affairs when foreigners and domestic citizens have entered and left the country. Customs documents the travel movements in the Travel Directory.[116]

Customs informs the Integration Agency[117] that the foreigners announced by the Ministry of Foreign Affairs have entered.

---

115 Ministry of Foreign Affairs - 4.7 Embassies
116 Ministry of Foreign Affairs - 4.8 Travel Directory
117 Ministry of Integration - 5 Integration Agency

The Integration Office[118] informs Customs which foreigners are obliged to leave the country and after what period they are to be forcibly deported by Customs. Customs informs the Integration Office when the foreigners have departed or have been deported .[119]

The Ministry of Health informs Customs which goods and services may not be imported or exported, or only to a limited extent, in order to protect the environment and health.[120]

The Ministry of Finance informs Customs which companies or persons are suspected of tax evasion or undeclared work.[121] The Customs tax investigators cooperate with the tax auditors in the search. The taxes collected are transferred to the Ministry of Finance. The monetary fines imposed flow to the Ministry of Security.

The auditors of the Company Auditing Agency[122] inform the Tax Investigation Department of Customs if they suspect undeclared work. In addition, all users of the Labour Directory[123] can also anonymously report undeclared work in their industry and indicate points or perimeters on the virtual map in the Security Directory where the Tax Investigation Department should take action.

The Ministry of Justice reports via the Court Directory[124] all convicted offenders who are either not allowed to enter or not allowed to leave the country.

The ministries of economy inform Customs of the import and export restrictions that apply to their respective economic forms and that companies must comply with.[125]

---

118 Ministry of Integration - 5.2.1 Integration Office
119 Ministry of Integration - 7.9.3 Deportation
120 Ministry of Health - 4.5.4 Institute of Environmental Health
121 Ministry of Finance - 5.7 Company Auditing Agency tax auditors
122 Ministry of Labor - 20 Company Auditing Agency
123 Ministry of Labour - 13 Labour Directory
124 Ministry of Justice - 5.5 Court Directory
125 Ministries of Economy - Switching between economic forms, Foreign trade

9.2 Border protection[126]

Customs is responsible for land, sea and air border control and controls for this purpose at border posts located at roads, ports and airports. Customs is supported by the military in border surveillance away from the border posts. Customs is primarily guided by the local police in border control. If the local police detect crimes in which the offenders have crossed the domestic borders, Customs protects the border with that country in consultation with the local police. Secondly, Customs is governed by the international union[127] , such as the European Union. This means that the security of citizens outweighs freedom through the unification of states. According to this principle, border controls can be introduced temporarily to protect the security of the population.

9.2.1 Ports and airports

At ports or airports, persons pass through a border post in the terminal. There, cameras record the face and radio sensors record the chip in the identity card or passport. If both match the data in the Persons Directory and Travel Directory, the glass doors open. Otherwise, a customs officer carries out a personal control.

9.2.2 Roads and rails

For vehicles on roads and rails, it is sufficient for all occupants to look out through the window and hold their identity card in their hands. The cameras immediately perform facial recognition. Additional thermal imaging cameras detect whether the number of faces detected matches the number of people on the thermal image. The vehicles and trains pass through a short control section where a frequency field is set up to detect the chips in the identity cards. During this pass, the vehicles are not allowed to drive faster than 80 km/h. If data was not recognised or there is a suspicion from the

---

126§173,2 Army: BV Art. 58
127Ministry of Foreign Affairs - 5.8 International Union

automatic data comparison, the vehicle must be controlled at a border post. Customs officers board trains at the next station and control the suspicious persons. Only once all these persons have been found may the doors of the train be opened.

After the automatic border checkpoints on roads, there are signs indicating the car number plate that must take the next exit in order to drive to the next border post or police station. This route is signposted and cameras are mounted on the signs to monitor the route from the border to the customs post or police station without any gaps. If the vehicle leaves this route or persons get out or goods are unloaded, an APB is immediately triggered and the licence plate number is entered in the Investigation Directory.

9.2.3 Airspace

Flying automobiles wishing to land inland must land in front of a border point and pass through the border point. At some border points there is also a camera system and a chip detection system, which is suspended in the air by helium balloons on ropes and must be flown through individually by the flying automobiles.

If the data could not be acquired, the pilot is radioed and must approach the next border checkpoint on a road, land and drive through. If problems arise again, the pilot must drive to the next border post. If the person is not allowed entry, landing inland is prohibited by radio. Overflight may also be prohibited. To force missiles to turn back or land, remote-controlled drones are launched that attach themselves to the missile. Military fighter jets force the aircraft to land or leave the airspace. In case of danger to local residents, the aircraft can be shot down if the plane does not comply with Customs' instructions.

9.2.4 Entry of persons

Customs is responsible for the entry of persons and maintains border posts with customs officers and identity check machines for this purpose. The checks on persons are mainly carried out automatically. Only if problems arise or if there is a suspicion of a criminal offence do customs officers control border crossers personally. They carry out the steps of the identity check machine manually. Only persons who can show a valid identity card or passport and, if applicable, a visa may enter the country.[128]

Customs checks the data of all persons entering and departing the country personally or automatically against the Travel Directory, Investigation Directory, Court Directory, Integration Directory and the Asylum Directory. If the persons are not authorised to enter or if an arrest warrant has been issued, they are arrested or forced to leave the country. Departure is forced by arrest and immediate removal behind the national border. Means of transport are confiscated and dropped off by customs officers at the same place behind the national border. The monetary fine is equivalent to the cost of the forced departure. If it cannot be paid, the amount must be worked off in detention.

9.2.4.1 Identity check machine

At border crossings on roads, ports or airports, there are identity check machines for the automatic registration of persons entering the country. The identity check machines consist of cameras for facial recognition and readers that remotely capture the chip in the identity card or passport in a short time. The captured face is compared with the passport photo and the person's data with the Persons Directory or Travel Directory.

Nationals have a profile in the Persons Directory. The chip in their identity card or passport contains a link to the holder's profile. Foreigners from International Union member states and third countries have a profile in the Travel Directory and

---

128 Ministry of Foreign Affairs - 4.7.3.4 Visa

a link to the chip in their identity card or customs sticker. The Travel Directory is used by Customs to make entries in profiles. Each traveller automatically receives a profile upon entry or a digital stamp with place, time and date in his or her existing profile.

All domestic and European identity cards contain a chip that is registered at border crossings. This means that not all travellers in the International Union have to show their identity card in person at Customs. Those who do not have a chip in their identity card or passport that can be read by the identity check machine must go to a border post and have customs officers affix a customs sticker to their passport and have it stamped. The sticker contains a chip on which the passport data is stored.

The identity check machine contains a radio frequency sensor that recognises the chip in the identity card or passport and can identify it. In the case of nationals, the corresponding data record is retrieved from the People's Computer of the person leaving or entering the country. The chip provides information about which person has just entered or left the country. This data is automatically stored in the Travel Directory.

Cameras are installed in the identity check machines in order to be able to photograph persons. The photo is used to match the data of the biometric passport photo from the chip with the biometric data of the border crosser's face as well as with the profile picture from the Persons Directory and Travel Directory. All persons crossing the border should look into the camera and hold their identity card or passport in their hand.

Persons who are not recognised, who can be assigned to more than one identity card or whose entry or departure is prohibited are advised to report immediately to the next border post with a customs officer. The recognised data is automatically reported to Customs and included in the Investigation Directory until the persons have been personally controlled by Customs officers.

9.2.5 Entry of foreigners

Persons entering from third countries outside the International Union must go to the nearest border post manned by customs officers when they enter for the first time. Customs will check the identity of the entrants there and, if necessary, check the visa with the embassy[129] in that country.

A stamp is entered into the passport of the entry and a customs sticker with chip function is affixed. The technology in the sticker comes from anti-theft devices from the retail sector, which are attached to goods and read out via sensors at the exit. This enables the identity check machines at the roads, ports and airports to register the departure and any further entry and exit.

Foreigners who have lost or forgotten their passports must wait until a staff member of their embassy picks them up and issues them temporary passports. Short-term detention at a local police station is permitted for this purpose.

Foreigners whose identity card has been taken away from them by their home country must go to an embassy in their home country or a neighbouring country of their home country and apply for asylum inland. Customs reports the entry of asylum seekers to the responsible Embassy and Integration Office.[130]

9.2.6 Entry bans

Criminal foreigners are not allowed entry into the inland. This is ensured by the embassies requesting police clearance certificates from the home countries before issuing a visa. Nationals from the International Union who have once been in detention inland are to be turned away at the border. Anyone who has been deported from the inland as a criminal foreigner and tries to re-enter, even as a tourist, is placed in detention and must work in detention until the price of the repatriation ticket has been developed. After that, he is deported again.

---

129 Ministry of Foreign Affairs - 4.7 Embassies
130 Ministry of Foreign Affairs - 9 Asylum application procedure,
Ministry of Integration - 8.4 Asylum procedure, 7.6.1 Entry

9.2.7 Entry restrictions

Foreigners who want to stay inland for longer than 12 months apply for this at the embassy in their home country. If the motions are approved, the foreigner receives his temporary guest ID card[131] at the embassy in his home country. There, the photo for the temporary identity card is taken, fingerprints are taken, the iris is scanned and stored on the identity card. These data are newly controlled inland by Customs or in the town hall. The original guest ID cards are available at any town hall, are only valid for the duration of stay and must be returned to the town hall or Customs on departure. If lost or taken away, compensation must be paid or a lifelong ban on entering the inland will be imposed.

All foreigners who remain inland for less than 12 months are not subject to the quota of foreigners. If the quota of foreigners[132] is reached for the whole country, no further visas or other entry permits are issued by the embassies. Foreigners are then turned back at the domestic borders.

9.2.8 Departure of persons

All persons, except for offenders in ongoing proceedings or prisoners, may leave the country at any time. The People's Computer may not be carried on departure. The identity card or passport must be carried. On departure, border checkpoints record who is leaving the country and when. This data is entered in the Travel Directory.

When foreigners depart, their identity must also be established. Foreigners whose identity card or passport does not have a chip in it that the border control points can recognise, or who have had Customs stickers affixed to them upon entry, must report to Customs in person. Those who do not do so commit a criminal offence and risk not being allowed to enter the inland. Customs staff carry out deportations in cooperation with the Integration Agency.[133]

---

131 Ministry of Integration - 4.4.1.4 Guest card
132 Ministry of Integration - 7.4 Quota of foreigners
133 Ministry of Integration - 7.9 Exit procedures

9.2.9 Goods inspections

The control of goods takes place at ports and airports on all vehicles and aircraft without exception. On roads it is only carried out on trucks and vans, on rails only on goods trains. Trucks and vans must visit a border post with a border control machine to cross the border. For all vehicles without exception, goods checks are only carried out at the external borders of the International Union.

The Ministry of Finance regulates the import and export of capital in voting with the ministries of economy.

9.2.9.1 Goods inspection machine

Goods inspection machines are capable of automatically scanning luggage, vehicles and freight containers and recognising the goods inside. This detects whether tariffs are due on the goods, what the goods are and whether there are any goods that are subject to prohibitions or restrictions. The data is stored in the Travel Directory in the profile of the traveller or transporter and compared with each other during entry and export.

The goods inspection machines are set up at ports, airports, border stations and long-distance border roads and vary in size depending on the type of use. If they generate harmful radiation, humans and certain animals are not allowed to pass through the goods inspection machine, only their outer clothing, luggage and cargo containers. Vehicles drive onto a conveyor belt, the occupants get out, walk around the goods inspection machine, get back into the vehicle and drive on. The process is similar to a car wash. Goods trains pass through the goods inspection machines, which are switched on after the railcar.

If conspicuous features are detected, customs officers subject the affected items to a personal control. If tariffs payments are due, the amount must be paid electronically at the goods inspection machine.

9.2.10 Import of goods

The import of goods by private persons is permitted in quantities customary in the household, provided the goods are not intended for sale. Commercial import of goods is permitted for companies from the Planned Economy, Social Market Economy and Free Market Economy. Customs duties are payable on imported goods. The amount of tariffs depends on the economic form in which the importing company is registered and the requirements from the Ministry of Finance.[134]

No consumer goods may be imported into Planned Economy, only raw materials, semi-finished products and tools. Only ecologically sustainable consumer goods, raw materials, semi-finished products and tools may be imported into the Social Market Economy. In the Free Market Economy, all goods may be imported that have been declared harmless and safe for the environment and human health.[135]

Goods may only be imported if they have a seal of approval from the technical auditors. Imported goods must receive and bear the CE seal.[136] Drugs may only be imported if they comply with the purity law .[137]

Counterfeits, lethal weapons, perishable or open foodstuffs, animals or plants and other goods that could introduce pathogens or foreign seeds may not be imported. In these cases, Customs receives the necessary requirements from the Institute of Environmental Medicine.[138]

Customs conducts People's Committees when deciding whether to allow or ban the import of certain goods. For example, the import of genetically modified food could be banned or prohibited only for the Social Market Economy.

---

134 Ministry of Finance - 5.3 Tariffs
135 Ministry of Labour - 20.7.6.4 Compliance with trade law
136 Ministry of Labour - 20.7.4.2 Seal of approval
137 Ministry of Health - 5.11.2 Purity Law
138 Ministry of Health - 4.5.4 Institute of Environmental Health

9.2.11 Import of capital

The import of capital must be declared to Customs and must pay duty on it in the same way as goods. Only the general VAT rate of 20% of the value applies here, regardless of whether the import of capital is carried out by companies or persons. The ministries of economy may enact additional requirements or levies as law.

9.2.12 Export of goods

The export of goods by private individuals is permitted to the extent customary in the household. Commercial export of goods is only permitted for companies from the Social Market Economy and Free Market Economy. Customs duties are payable on exported goods. The amount of the tariffs depends on the current VAT rate. The Company Auditing Agency's legality auditors check compliance with commercial law, in particular compliance with export bans.[139]
Only high quality, durable or pure goods may be exported from the Social Market Economy. Goods that have been tested by customers or the Company Auditing Agency's technical auditors as „not durable for quality reasons" and thus have not received a seal of approval[140] are banned from export.
All goods may be exported from the Free Market Economy without any conditions. All weapons are excluded from this. Weapons may only be supplied to state security agencies of states with which there is a defence alliance and a peace treaty.

9.2.13 Export of capital

Customs tariffs of 20% apply to the export of capital, i.e. money or assets, by private individuals who are also nationals. Customs duties apply to companies in the Social Market Economy and Free Market Economy. The export of capital is prohibited in the Planned Economy and Barter Economy. Foreigners who work inland and send money abroad are subject

---

139 Ministry of Labour - 20.7.6.4 Compliance with trade law
140 Ministry of Labour - 17.7.4 Seal of approval

to 60% tariffs, foreign companies to 40%. The background to this is that the export of capital from the domestic market reduces purchasing power here and thus also the standard of living at home. Therefore, export duties are levied on foreign remittances to compensate for the loss of purchasing power. The same applies to dividends from shares whose shareholders live abroad and take the dividends earned inland out of the country.

9.3 Tax Investigation Department

The Tax Investigation Department is a department of Customs. It works closely with the Ministry of Finance, but also with all necessary ministries. The Tax Investigation Department operates mainly inland, but also abroad. It also checks the import and export of capital. It specialises in the financial control of money flows within the country and with foreigners and has a right of information vis-à-vis all banks operating inland. In addition, the Customs Tax Investigation Department carries out controls in companies and households to uncover undeclared work.

9.3.1 Tax Investigation abroad

If taxes are evaded abroad or with the help of foreigners, Customs becomes active and works together with the embassy in the affected country.[141] Foreign trips by Tax Investigation Departments should be possible in exceptional cases, but the rule is that they are handled by the embassy staff in that country. Extradition requests, payment orders, entry bans or economic trade restrictions can be applied for by Customs at the embassies after a domestic court issues the order. The court proceedings are conducted in the absence of the fugitive culprit. The order requires the Ministry of Foreign Affairs with its embassies to contact the affected politicians in the country to implement the measures ordered. The Minister of Foreign Affairs has the final decision-making right here for punitive

---

141 Ministry of Foreign Affairs - 4.7 Embassies

measures against another country. To the extent that the other country cooperates, no or harsh entry bans and economic restrictions will be imposed. If the other country covers up tax fraud, all trade and movement of persons with the inland can be banned.

9.3.1.1 Tax evasion abroad

At the external borders, the export and import of cash is controlled and the banknotes are stored in a register to better simulate the money supply. Specialists work for the electronic transfer of money in the capital city of the Ministry of Security. They use algorithms to check the international transfer of money from and to the domestic market.

9.3.2 Domestic Tax Investigation

Domestic taxes are evaded through transactions that are managed outside the tax account at the People's Bank.[142] All business transactions involving cash must be deposited by the recipient through a cash register[143] after settlement. The private transfer of cash within the family or circle of friends is not taxed, as here the transaction takes place in the confidence that the recipient will use it to purchase a good or service in the giver's interest. For example, people may give each other money or buy something together. The tax deduction of 20% at the ATM is intended to cover all private investments for consumption. It is not decisive for tax purposes whether a person, a family or a group of friends consumes together. The Tax Investigation Department follows up on anomalies and can initiate open or undercover investigations.

---

142 Ministry of Finance - 11 People's Bank, 5.5 Tax Account
143 Ministry of Finance - 5.2.3 Cash

9.3.2.1 Cash control

For digital control, the numbers on the banknotes are recorded when the money is withdrawn and assigned to the person who withdrew the money. Companies that accept cash for remuneration must deposit this money into the company account via the cash register. Here, too, the numbers on the banknotes are recorded. Now the path of the money can be calculated digitally. This data flows to the Ministry of Finance to determine the velocity of money in circulation.[144] The programme always shows suspicious money flows, all other money flows are deleted. The People's Innovation Company Intranet creates the programme.[145] The Tax Investigation Department uses the data to investigate the black market and identify offenders.

9.3.2.2 Moonlighting

The Tax Investigation Department for undeclared work focuses on persons or companies that accept cash for goods or services. The cash from private investments in goods and services is to be taxed as income of companies with the business tax.
If there is a suspicion of undeclared work, i.e. tax that has not been paid or not been paid correctly, this can be reported to the Tax Investigation Department. Every police station accepts suspicious activity reports from citizens. Suspicious activity reports from the legality auditors of the Company Auditing Agency[146] are received directly by the Tax Investigation Department. The Tax Investigation Department investigates and observes the reported case. To avoid lengthy observation, surveillance is carried out by video and drone or satellite.
In case of suspicion of trade on the black market, cameras are set up in companies to film the buyers and sellers during trade. If there are deviations from the previously taxed income, the video surveillance is continued for 5 years. Usually, the entrepreneurs know about the installation of the cameras. In

---

144 Ministry of Finance - 10.7.1 Quantity equation of money
145 Ministry of Digital Affairs - 13 People's Innovation Company Intranet
146 Ministry of Labour - 20.7.6.5 Tax Investigation Department

order to be able to carry out a covert investigation with hidden cameras in the company, a judge must issue the order for this. If undeclared work is suspected, services are observed by video surveillance. Areas and buildings where undeclared workers are supposed to perform services are monitored from the air. This way, all persons entering and leaving an area or building are detected. All persons are detected by facial recognition with hidden installed ground cameras.

10 Military[147]

The military is responsible for defending the country and its people against attacks from abroad and from outer space. It protects the external borders and critical infrastructure inland. To do this, it deploys an army consisting of salaried soldiers, able-bodied citizens, analogue and digital weapon systems. The supreme commander of the military is the Minister of Security in voting with the people. The military is divided into a professional army of the European Defence Army and an army based on the militia principle with soldiers who are employed in the People's Protection Service or other gainful employment in peacetime.

In the short and medium term, the military is still needed to defend against human attacks. In the long term, humans should stop fighting each other militarily through diplomacy and democracy. In the long term, the military should defend the Earth as the homeland of humanity against extraterrestrial interference and, if necessary, conquer other planets.

The case of a foreign mission of the military is only permissible if the external borders threaten to be overrun by the enemy in war. All other foreign missions are prohibited.

10.1 Militia principle

In peacetime, citizens learn new weapons systems in military exercises. They practise action in war, civil war, coup d'état, revolts and coups at least once every 10 years. The military

---

147§169,7 Security, §173,1,2,5 Army: BV Art. 58, 173, §172,3 Internal and external security in state of emergency

protecting the inland varies in size in times of peace and in times of war. In times of peace, soldiers on standby in the European Defence Army secure the borders and the country against ambushes. All other soldiers trained in current weapons systems work in the People's Protection Service or elsewhere on alert.

10.2 State of emergency

In a state of emergency, the Minister of Security deploys the domestic military to put an end to war, civil war, revolts and coups as quickly as possible.[148] In the event of a state of siege and widespread counterattack, all nationals between the ages of 20 and 60 who are fit for military service are conscripted. Soldiers from the People's Protection Service will be given leadership duties. Weapons are issued to the rest of the population who remain in their homeland to defend themselves. Every nationals undergoes basic military training during the People's Service and is thus made fit for military service.

In the event of a coup d'état[149] all soldiers are ordered by the constitution and this law to disobey the commander-in-chief. During a coup d'état, the commander-in-chief takes power away from the people, so soldiers must refuse to obey him. Instead, they are to steal implements of war and use them to join the vigilantes. Vigilantes are under the supreme command of the respective municipality's mayor. The mayor exercises supreme command over a vigilante in voting with the citizens of his municipality.

10.3 Allies

The Ministry of Security, in voting with the Ministry of Foreign Affairs, endeavours to jointly defend the common external borders with allied neighbouring states in an International Union. To this end, the member states jointly

---

148 Ministry of State Organisation - 12.7.3 War, 12.7.4 Civil War, 12.7.5 Revolt, 12.7.6 Coup
149 Ministry of State Organisation - 12.7.7 Coup d'état

operate modern defence facilities at the external borders and against celestial bodies with their armies. Military service to operate the defence facilities is only triggered in the event of an attack. All soldiers then immediately occupy their posts at the weapon systems and all citizens carry out the orders they have learned in basic training and practised regularly.

10.3.1 European Defence Army[150]

The domestic army allies itself with all armies of the European Union member states to form a European Defence Army. This military alliance must be agreed to by a majority of all peoples of all member states before it enters into force. All member states of the European Defence Army must have peace treaties with each other and agree on laws with the peoples involved. In the laws, they regulate joint action in the event of defence, military exercises, standby services at defence installations and weapon systems, as well as the financing of the European Defence Army.

In order to be able to build and operate defence facilities in strategically necessary locations, affected municipalities may be relocated, soldiers settled or the development changed. The Ministry of Security is responsible for providing compensation in voting with the affected citizens.

The best weapon systems and the best soldiers are deployed from the member states to the European Defence Army on standby. Various strategies will be devised for the defence of the European continent by land, sea and air. On the European Union's external borders, defensive positions are being built against ground forces, and on the coasts, defensive positions against landing forces. Within the continent, laser and missile defence shields protect cities and strategically important communication routes and supply facilities against attacks of any kind from the air. The emplacements blend architecturally into the landscape and are sealed with hatches that are armoured and coloured to match the external environment. The army of soldiers is so large that all defensive installations can be

---

150 §173,3 Army, §175,2,3 Organisation, training and equipment of the army: BV Art. 60

manned and able-bodied citizens serve as reinforcements. Weapon systems are being researched and acquired that are capable of detecting, attacking or deflecting celestial bodies. If possible, the defence systems should be able to be used to defend the country's borders and the earth. In the medium term, the national defence installations and the mobile troops for land, sea and air will be automated and remotely controlled. In the long term, all military troops should be able to defend the earth against extraterrestrial influences. To this end, all armies should ally to form a global defence army and work together to discover and colonise other Earth-like planets. The European Defence Army is prohibited from wars of aggression and the use of armed force abroad, unless that foreign country is attacking European territory. Terrorist attacks by foreign terrorist organisations are resolved diplomatically by no longer supporting the cause of the terror.

10.3.2 European secret service

Since it is rarely clear whether a terrorist organisation or a foreigner's secret service is behind an attack, the European Defence Army has special task forces. They are specialised in spying on heads of state who are waging a war of aggression against European territory and terror chiefs who occupy key positions in a terror organisation that has carried out attacks in Europe, and if necessary to kidnap or deliberately kill them and dispose of the bodies. The mafia is also considered a terrorist organisation, i.e. organisational structures that resemble companies but are not registered in the Labour Directory and engage in illegal trade, for example in humans, weapons or contract killings. The task forces operate in secret and receive their orders from the police investigating agencies.

10.4 Soldiers[151]

All soldiers together form the army. Soldier law stipulates that soldiers, uniformed and armed, may not assemble without orders to do so. The right of assembly is accordingly restricted for them. Soldiers are either professional soldiers, reserve soldiers, reservists or citizens fit for military service, who are deployed in accordance with the following military law.

Professional soldiers of the European Defence Army permanently staff the defence facilities and maintain the devices. Reserve soldiers are permanently employed by the People's Protection Service and only do their service as soldiers in a state of emergency. Reservists are voluntary citizens who, after their basic training, still participate regularly in shooting and military exercises. In the event of war, all domestic nationals who have completed basic training, are between 20 and 60 years of age and are in good health are required to perform military service. All other domestic nationals will be required to perform military service in the war economy. In the event of a coup d'état, citizens and deserted soldiers contribute to the civil defence of the constitution in vigilantes. Soldiers may and must desert in the event of a coup d'état by defying the unconstitutional orders of the commander-in-chief and joining a vigilante.

Soldiers who are not permanently employed and who participate in basic training, military exercises or war missions receive military pay equivalent to the revenues from their other gainful employment. Soldiers who suffer damage to their health during deployment receive the best possible health care. Surviving dependants of soldiers killed in action receive pension payments from the Ministry of Security equivalent to the last income paid.

---

151 §174,4,5 Military and People's Service: BV Art.59, §172,2e Internal and external security in state of emergency

10.4.1 Basic training[152]

All nationals must complete basic training and military exercises. Basic training takes place during the first three months in the People's Service[153] . Basic training includes mustering, theoretical and practical training for national defence and for the People's Protection Service. Military exercises are conducted on a regular basis and are integrated into basic training. Soldiers and reservists attend the military exercises by returning to the place of their basic training and conducting exercises together with the People's Service workers.

10.4.1.1 Mustering

At the muster in the nearest Social Village, military tactical fitness for the various weapon systems is tested. Depending on fitness, more physically demanding responsibilities are assigned. Wishes may be expressed for a weapon system or a troop type, but whether forces are still needed there or elsewhere is decided by the military personnel administration programme of the digital administration[154] . Those who do not wish to perform service with weapons must indicate this at muster and will be assigned to non-weapon military services. Those who refuse service with a weapon nevertheless learn to shoot. This is to enable them to better protect themselves against attacks because they know how they work.

10.4.1.2 Training

The theoretical training is about the military organisational structure, which is hierarchical. Here, command and obedience apply. Orders that violate the constitution must be reported to the public prosecutor's office[155] . Ranks indicate

---

152§173,1,5 Army: BV Art. 58, 173, §174,1,2 Military and People's Service: BV Art. 59, §172,3 Internal and external security in a state of emergency
153Ministry of Education - 10 People's Service
154Ministry of Digital Affairs - 5 Digital Administration
155Ministry of Justice - 5.6.3.1 Charges against security agencies

the position in the hierarchy. Clear areas of accountability and reliable proper execution of orders are taught. In defence tactics lessons, the interaction of weapon systems is explained and how and where the domestic or European borders can be defended most effectively.

The practical training is characterised by obstacle courses with baggage and orienteering marches with baggage, position battles, ambushes, self-defence, roadblocks, object protection, equipment pick-up and care, as well as work on the weapon system for which one was assigned in the muster. The weapon system decides the location of basic training so that sufficient training objects can be provided. The recruits learn to manage and maintain the weapon system.

During basic training, all nationals learn how to shoot. Practice is done with the weapon groups for small arms, i.e. pistol, submachine gun, rifle, machine gun, sniper rifle, bazooka or rocket launcher. The use of hand grenades is also practised.

Basic training also includes training for the People's Protection Service. The reason for this is that soldiers are supposed to behave justly towards the civilian population during the war, so that volunteers can work for the People's Protection Service at any time after basic training.

10.4.2 Weapon systems[156]

The Ministry of Security provides for the proper equipment of up-to-date weapon systems capable of repelling enemy attacks and defending the earth against celestial bodies. The financing and installation of geostationary defence systems is undertaken in voting with the Ministry of Foreign Affairs together with other states.

In the short term, the best available weapon systems of all member states will be used by the European Defence Army, operated and maintained by trained soldiers. All of Europe will be covered by missile and laser defence shields against various missiles.

In the medium term, all weapon systems on land, sea and

156§175,1,4 Organisation, training and equipment of the armed forces: BV Art. 60

in the air will be remote-controlled. Here it is important to ensure protection against EMP attacks. The electromagnetic waves destroy all digital systems that are not specially secured. EMP bombs are the first explosive devices to be dropped over enemy territory in order to paralyse the country without having to kill humans.

In the long term, there should be no more weapons systems that can kill humans. In the long term, it will be necessary to ward off bombardment from space. This includes comets, meteorites or planets that are on a collision course in Earth's orbit. Weapon systems should also be available for extraterrestrial life forms. But to keep weapons on Earth for this, even though all of humanity is finally living in peace, is not worth it. It is necessary to recognise potential intelligent alien attackers before they perceive and attack the Earth. In a pinch, there is still the armament that the police have at their disposal. Heavy weapon systems are in Earth orbit and must not be directed at Earth because humanity would not survive that.

10.5 Warfare[157]

The Minister of Security is responsible for waging war in voting with the people. Voting with the people is precautionary in peacetime and regular in wartime. For precautionary voting, laws are enacted and votes are taken on how warfare is to be shaped and organised. This includes how war crimes are prevented, investigated and reported.[158]

After the start of a war, the Minister of Security calls a voting within 2 weeks on whether the war should continue. If the war is expected to last longer than 3 weeks, a committee must be held one day after the voting. Depending on the voting result, negotiations are held on how the war should be ended or continued. As long as the war lasts, a voting must be held every 3 months on whether the war should continue or whether the security minister should submit the surrender.

---

157 §173,4 Army: BV Art. 58, §172,2a,4 Internal and external security in a state of emergency
158 Ministry of Justice - 8.13.9 War crimes

The veto quorum against the war or the conduct of the war is regarded as a further means of co-determination by the people. As soon as the Security Minister prepares the declaration of war, he opens a profile for it in the Legislative Directory. Here, citizens can already veto the text of the declaration of war. Veto quorums against war, unlike other quorums, must be accompanied by a request, like petitions.[159] As soon as 50% of the people support the quorum, a committee is convened, or if the request only contains a voting question, a vote is held.

10.5.1 Digital war

The Ministry of Digital Affairs supports the military with its best experts, data and computer programmes for digital crime.[160] Soldiers who report for digital weapon systems are trained accordingly by the Ministry of Education and further trained by the Ministry of Digital Affairs for digital crime.

In cooperation with the Institute for Information Security, the most damaging and effective digital attacks and spies are identified and further developed. These weapons are used against attackers. With successful analytical methods from cyber defence, the attackers are tracked down and kidnapped or killed with military or intelligence means.

In regular exercises, the military tries to circumvent the defences of domestic digital systems in order to attack or spy on them. They report their successes to the Ministry of Digital Affairs, which contacts those affected so that data protection can be improved. If there are no suitable defences for the digital weapons, they are developed in cooperation with the People's Innovation Company Intranet. The military can keep its weapons and attacks secret for tactical reasons, but must then ensure that at least the state infrastructure is protected against the weapons and attacks.

---

159 Ministry of State Organisation - 9.10.11.6 Petition
160 Ministry of Digital Affairs - 8 Digital Crime

10.5.2 Coup[161]

The military, together with the police, is advancing with appropriate weapon systems to the borders of the areas occupied by armed coup plotters. All means of access to the area are sealed off. The military units capture houses and roads one by one along several corridors through the city. Through the corridors, unarmed residents of the municipality are evacuated several times a day by armoured vehicles and taken to reception camps in surrounding municipalities. The disaster management is responsible for the construction and operation of the reception camps. There is no attack on the municipality. All supplies of food, water, electricity, telecommunications and other supplies to the municipality are cut off. This state of affairs is maintained until the insurgents are weak or out of ammunition, so that they cannot withstand an assault. In the event of a storming, sleeping gas is to be used if possible to avoid open firefights. Coup plotters are disarmed, arrested and handed over to the court.[162]

If hostages are taken by insurgents during a state of siege, negotiations are held with the hostage-takers. The aim is always to free as many hostages as possible. Concessions and the fulfilment of the hostage-takers' wishes should be made in such a way that the means made available are sabotaged and do more damage than good to the hostage-takers.

10.5.3 Defence war[163]

If a state attacks the national borders of a member state of the European Defence Army, war is declared against that state. Wars of aggression are prohibited. The Ministry of Security must also declare war at the latest when war has been declared on a European Defence Army member state. As soon as the domestic territory is affected by a declaration of war, martial law is declared.

All nationals put themselves on alert for a marching order.

---

161 §172.2d Internal and external security in a state of emergency
162 Ministry of Justice - 8.14.5.3 Coup
163 §172.2a Internal and external security in a state of emergency

This means that they can be at a designated place within 30 minutes, fully equipped. Some of their equipment is stored at home and weapons are stored at the local police station. To be fully alert, they go to the police station and receive their designated weapons and ammunition. These are the weapons that citizens have already used during the exercises, but this time with live ammunition. In war, the people carry deadly weapons to defend themselves. If the enemy arrives with lethal weapons and threatens the interior of the country, they should know that they will find a population there that is able to defend itself.

All persons who are unfit for combat and easily vulnerable, such as the elderly, the disabled and children, are removed from the front line affected by combat operations. They are either moved to sparsely populated parts of the country or to countries with appropriate reception agreements. Such reception agreements are already agreed with all neighbouring states in peacetime. Accommodation in rural areas or in other countries is provided by host families. Those who report as host families state how many persons they can accommodate and receive state compensation for the care they provide. Host families are part of the warfare and are already assigned their roles in the exercises.

All soldiers are immediately deployed to the defences, all citizens fit for military service are deployed as required and receive a marching order to do so. They must then present themselves at the designated place and can use all public transport free of charge for this purpose. They carry their weapons with them at all times. All weapons and remaining ammunition are confiscated after the war. The issue of weapons and ammunition is entered in the national weapons register and signed out again when they are returned. Missing weapons and conspicuously high consumption of ammunition are investigated by the police. Persons who retain weapons or ammunition are liable to prosecution.

All companies are converting their activities to a war economy, as has already been rehearsed in the exercises. All citizens who are not needed in combat do their service in the war economy.

10.5.3.1 War of position

In the event of a hostile siege of the external borders, the defence strategy depends on the range of fire into the domestic territory. Up to 50 kilometres to the front is acceptable. If the shelling extends further into the European mainland, it is fired correspondingly far into the enemy's interior. This only applies to a war on external land borders. The air force, with its aircraft and air defence positions, is responsible for the air. It is supposed to guarantee air sovereignty over European airspace. The navy is responsible for the water. Since Europe has the longest external borders by water, the navy is the strongest troop category. It prevents all enemy troop movements at sea, sinks warships and captures enemy supply ships. Attacking states are only attacked by bombs and missiles throughout their entire national borders when defensive installations are in danger of being destroyed, overrun or captured.

10.5.3.2 Analogue war

In the event of an area-wide attack by an electromagnetic pulse (EMP), there will be a switch to classic analogue warfare. Although the defence facilities are largely shielded against EMP attacks, they are also designed for analogue warfare. Weapons and ammunition without computer chips are stored. The population is mainly equipped with analogue weapons and can defend their territory accordingly. Positions are taken up along the external borders, but also everywhere in the country, and checkpoints are established. For this eventuality, the basic training also includes practising classical national defence, including navigation with map and compass, as well as drawing up maps and building positions and checkpoints. The citizens are supported by experienced reservists and receive a compass and a soldier's handbook in addition to their weapon. The manual summarises the basic training and describes how to behave in the event of war.

11 Switching to the new system

The Ministry of Security takes over the Ministry of Defence and reduces it to its new tasks inland and at the national borders. From the Ministry of the Interior, it takes over the tasks of maintaining public safety and order, prevention of danger and disaster management. Once the regions are dissolved, all duplications are combined and all areas of accountability are filled.

11.1 No private security services

Private security services are banned. The monopoly on the use of force must be exercised by the democratically governed state, not by companies or even joint-stock companies. The People's Protection Service replaces private security companies and building protectors who use armed security personnel. Security personnel who are unarmed but are expected to use force in an emergency must also be provided by the People's Protection Service. Companies that need to employ personnel to protect themselves from physical violence by their customers must purchase this protection service from the People's Protection Service and not from private security services. Only the directly democratically elected security minister or his deputy with his security forces may use force.

A People's Committee establishes the rules for security and public order. These rules also determine how serious offences are and with what severity they may be punished. Security forces are allowed to use physical force much earlier.

Employed People's Protection Officers are former soldiers or employees of private security services who want to switch to the People's Protection Service when they switch to the new system.

11.2 Distribution of tasks in the water rescue service

The state agencies for water rescue become the water rescue service, which takes over the protective service on inland and open sea waters.

11.3 Reorganisation of the criminal investigation department

The civil police is the new name of the criminal police. Until now, at least two police officers were needed for patrol duties. With the People's Protection Service, only one policeman is needed. The police officers available as a result are used for investigative activities in order to be able to solve more criminal cases.

11.4 Dissolution of the secret services

The best secret service agents and technologies from all European secret services will be pooled in the new European secret service. Former agents and workers of the national secret services can apply for the Special Operations Command, work in the Criminal Investigation Department and Digital Police or in the People's Protection Service. The foreigner and military secret services will be dissolved. The domestic intelligence service will be transformed into the Office for the Protection of the Constitution and will only monitor ministries, authorities, as well as their employees and politicians for their compliance with the Constitution.

11.5 Enlargement of NATO

The North Atlantic Treaty Organisation (NATO)[164] is seeking to admit Russia, India and China as soon as possible. For the purpose of global security, the coupling of democratic standards and participation in a defence alliance is waived. This will create a global defence alliance capable of avoiding a world war. In the medium term, at least all nuclear powers should be members of this global defence alliance. If NATO refuses to admit Russia or China, the European Union, for its part, should agree on a defence alliance with Russia and China, thus establishing the global defence alliance. The final decision on the entrance or exit of a state into or out of the global defence alliance is made by the people in a voting.

---

164   https://www.nato.int/

11.6 Consolidation of the military

The military and armies of the other member states will be merged into the European Defence Army. All troop types will be merged and the best weapon systems that can be used for military and civilian purposes will be retained. All other weapon systems will be converted for civilian use. Defence posts will be built on all coasts and external borders of the European Union and equipped with remotely controlled attack units by sea, land and air.

The army, air force and navy are divided among the participating member states and the best institutions and elite units are retained. If necessary, units will move to other barracks. All surplus combat equipment, such as missiles, ammunition or gun turrets, will be stored and reassembled in the event of war. In the case of tanks, turrets are replaced by turrets with excavators or cranes and used as construction vehicles.

All of Europe will be shielded by missile and laser defence shields against various missiles. Mobile combat forces will be reduced to operating up to 300 km beyond their own borders. Remote-controlled weapons represent higher initial investments but low follow-up costs. The aim should be that no European soldier has to fight abroad, but that in the event of an attack on the European Union's external border, only remote-controlled weapons fight enemy units in front of the border.

Voluntary member states begin the process of establishing the European Defence Army, which other member states can join, and holds a referendum in the affected countries for this purpose.

11.6.1 Use of the barracks

The reduction in the number of soldiers in barracks and the resulting barracks closures would cause job losses in the neighbouring settlements. Barracks, like military devices, are used for civilian purposes in peacetime. This is achieved by converting barracks into Social Villages, keeping the troop kitchen, laundry and medical squadron in operation, and moving social welfare recipients into the barracks. Gradually, former welfare recipients replace staff from military times. The number of people who lived and will live in the barracks is to be kept constant or increased.

All barracks are converted into Social Villages. The new residents help to decide how which rooms or localities are to be used. Hangars will be converted into factory buildings, residential buildings will be converted into apartment buildings. The conversion is managed by the Ministry of Planned Economy in voting with the Ministry of Security. This will ensure that the Social Villages can be quickly reused as barracks in the event of war.

11.7 Schengen area

The Schengen area with its border controls at the European Union's external borders will continue. Border protection is in the hands of the European Defence Army, once it exists. The domestic borders are only controlled by Customs when the police report cross-border criminals. This can be a section or the entire national border. If the protection of the European Union's external borders is inadequate, the domestic border is monitored by the military and customs officers control at border posts.

11.8 Import sales tax

Import turnover tax is replaced by Customs tariffs on the import of goods.

11.9 Conversion of the old ministries

All departments and units that transfer to the Ministry of Security are listed below. If only the department or sub-department is named, all its units are transferred. If individual units are named, only those units are transferred. All departments and units not named are dropped. Existing staff adapt their tasks to the new requirements. The corresponding names of the units can usually be found as keywords in the running text.

11.9.1 Foreign Office[165]

2 Policy Department
Policy issues and coordination of the European Union's Common Foreign and Security Policy (CFSP, including CSDP), Common Security and Defence Policy (CSDP), Franco-German Defence and Security Council, security policy relations with European Union Member States

11.9.2 Federal Ministry of Justice and Consumer Protection[166]

II Criminal law
Crime prevention, criminology

IV Constitutional and Administrative Law, International and European Law
Police law, soldier law, law of civil defence

11.9.3 Federal Ministry of Finance[167]

III Customs, sales tax, excise duties
Fiscal Code (Customs), controls, audits, enforcement, Customs Investigation Service, Central Financial Transaction Investigation Unit (FIU), criminal and administrative offences law, prohibitions and restrictions, financial control, moonlighting, European Union and international cooperation, administrative and legal assistance, foreign trade and payments law

---

165 https://www.auswaertiges-amt.de/blob/215270/004ca2ab6cbacdd63 78eee0eb8077417/organisationsplan-data.pdf Status: 17.05.2019
166 https://www.bmjv.de/SharedDocs/Downloads/DE/Ministerium/ Organisationsplan/Organisationsplan_DE.pdf;jsessionid=A807B5B1F5E FC74825E8B2A6508405BE.2_cid297?__blob=publicationFile&v=131 Viewed on: 14/05/2019
167 https://www.bundesfinanzministerium.de/Content/DE/Downloads/ Ministerium/organigramm.pdf?__blob=publicationFile&v=27 Status: 01.05.2019

Customs law and procedures, import turnover tax, market regulation law

11.9.4 Federal Ministry of the Interior, for Building and the Homeland[168]

ÖS Public Safety
Police and Law Enforcement, Police Information System, Data Protection in the Security Sector, BKA Law
Serious and organised crime inland, counterintelligence, ABC crime, economic protection, sabotage protection, parliamentary control committee, G 10, cyber security, terrorism/ extremism right/left, politically motivated crime

B Affairs of the Federal Police
Policy, legal, personnel and organisational matters of the police, technology and logistics, command and operational resources, command and operational matters of the police, riot police, maritime security, aviation security, information, communication technology, cyber capabilities of the police

KM Crisis Management and Civil Protection

11.9.5 Bavarian State Ministry of the Interior, for Sport and Integration[169]

C Public safety and order
Budget management, equipment and supply of the police, law of public safety and order, deployment of the police, information and communication systems of the police, basic matters of all BOS

D Fire brigade, rescue service and disaster management

E Constitutional protection, cyber security

168https://www.bmi.bund.de/SharedDocs/downloads/DE/ veroeffentlichungen/themen/ministerium/organigramm-bmi.html Status: 25.03.2019
169https://www.stmi.bayern.de/assets/stmi/min/organisation/201030_ organigramm_stmi_hausbrosch%C3%BCre.pdf Status: 30.10.2020

Weapons and assembly law, bans on associations

11.9.6 Federal Ministry of Defence[170]

A Equipment

CIT Cyber/Information Technology

FüSK Armed Forces Command

Social Market Economy I Military Intelligence, Personnel Structure

11.9.7 Federal Chancellery[171]

7 Federal Intelligence Service
Cyber intelligence, security, proliferation (spread of weapons of mass destruction), economic protection, organised crime, technical reconnaissance and cyber intelligence, crisis situations

---

170 https://www.bmvg.de/resource/blob/11902/0710c6355d3e95f 4c622d272db28e8cc/a-03-download-organigramm-data.pdf Status: 15.02.2021
171 https://www.bundesregierung.de/resource/blob/975196/773044/965 a4d1b633cb6529246be5f4b016d8d/druckversion-organigramm-bkamt-data.pdf?download=1 Status: 25.02.2021

Contact form

Dear reader
If you would like to make what you have read come true, in whole or in part, together with other like-minded people, I offer you several possibilities with this contact form. Fill it out, tear out the page and send it by post to:
Andreas Seidl, P.O. Box 1206, 63488 Seligenstadt / Germany

Or send the details to:
Phone: 0049 1522 818 2243 (whatsapp, telegram, signal)
Email: andreas.seidl2022@web.de

Please mark with a cross:
O   I want to found a dynamic People's Party.
O   I want to donate money for implementation.
O   I want contacts with like-minded people in my area.

Forename: ____

Surname: ____

Please fill in only the contact option through which a reply should be made.

Street, house no.:   _____________________________________

Postcode, city, country: _____________________________________

Phone: _____________________________________

Email address: _____________________________________